FUN & EASY SCROLL SAW PROJECTS

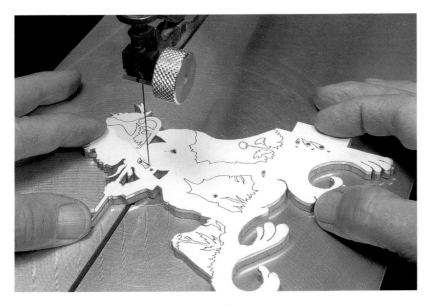

PATRICK SPIELMAN

Sterling Publishing Co., Inc,
New York

CIP Information Available

10 9 8 7 6 5 4 3 2

Published by Sterling Publishing Company, Inc.
387 Park Avenue South, New York, N.Y. 10016
© 2002 by Patrick Spielman
Distributed in Canada by Sterling Publishing
℅ Canadian Manda Group, One Atlantic Avenue, Suite 105
Toronto, Ontario, Canada M6K 3E7
Distributed in Australia by Capricorn Link (Australia) Pty Ltd.
P.O. Box 704, Windsor, NSW2756 Australia
Printed in China
All rights reserved
Sterling ISBN 0-8069-9399-5

ACKNOWLEDGMENTS

The author extends his most sincere gratitude to everyone who assisted with this book. A hearty thank you to the following individuals for providing original project designs, participating in shop help, or preparing the drawings and the manuscript:

Bragi Baldursson

Jennifer Blahnik

Dirk Boelman

Bev Carmody

Brian Dahlen

Gösta Dahlqvist

Karl Gutbrod

Gail Hathaway

Julie Kiehnau

Dean Larson

Roxanne LeMoine

Barbara & Harvey Malzahn

Barbara McGivern

Aaron Joel Moriarity

Kyle Oram

Herb Parsons

Cathy Peck

Dennis Phillips

Patricia Spielman

Robert Spielman

Karl Stubenvoll

Dale Taylor

R. Stephen Toman

Paula Zinngrabe Wendland

Joan West

Don Zinngrabe

CONTENTS

INTRODUCTION 5

CHAPTER 1
BASIC TECHNIQUES & INFORMATION 6

CHAPTER 2
QUICK & HANDY PROJECTS 14

CHAPTER 3
HOLIDAY ORNAMENTS 44

CHAPTER 4
CROSSES 72

CHAPTER 5
CUTOUTS & SILHOUETTES 86

CHAPTER 6
SHELVES 116

CHAPTER 7
CLOCKS 124

CHAPTER 8
CANDLESTICKS 140

CHAPTER 9
BOXES 146

CHAPTER 10
PERSONALIZED PROJECTS 158

CHAPTER 11
LOGSCAPES 166

CHAPTER 12
MISCELLANEOUS HOME ACCESSORIES 175

METRIC EQUIVALENCY CHART 190

INDEX 191

ABOUT THE AUTHOR 192

INTRODUCTION

In addition to project designs created by the author and his family, this book also includes original designs from more than 25 prominent scroll saw artists. It contains over 235 decorative and functional patterns for more than 100 projects, which are organized into 12 chapter categories. Almost all of the projects included here first appeared in Patrick Spielman's bimonthly newsletter/magazine, Home Workshop News, *published between 1995 and 2000. Many of the projects are ideal for the beginning scroll-sawer and can be made in an hour or less. Most do not require expert sawing skills, or large and expensive pieces of material. There are, however, a few projects that will challenge the beginner and entertain the experienced scroll-sawer.*

Scroll-sawers will see projects made from a variety of materials other than wood, including paper, plastic, and metal. Some interesting finishes are also introduced such as those that make wood look like brightly polished metal or metal to look as if it were aged to a beautiful turquoise patina.

If you are new to scroll-sawing and wish to learn more about the tools and techniques, refer to the author's best-selling books Scroll Saw Basics *and the* New Scroll Saw Handbook. *Additional projects and designs can be found in Spielman's more than 30 scroll saw pattern books, all of which are available from Sterling Publishing Company.*

BASIC TECHNIQUES
& INFORMATION

MATERIALS AND FINISHES

A wide variety of materials are available to make the projects in this book. Solid hardwoods and softwoods (**1–1**), a variety of plywoods and other wood-based sheet materials (**1–2**), paper, stiff cardboard, sheet metals, and a number of different plastics (**1–3**) are all now easily cutable with excellent results using the scroll saw. Determine what look you want before selecting the material. Obviously, it is not practical to paint expensive hardwoods such as walnut or cherry.

In many project situations, using an unconventional material will generate an entirely new look. A simple silhouette, for example, sawn from plastic or cut from wood and finished to look like metal, can be very stunning (**1–3** to **1–5**).

1–1. Solid softwoods such as this economical No. 2 shop pine are good materials for small projects that can be cut out between defects.

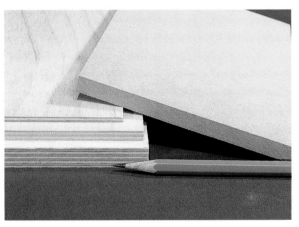

1–2. Good hardwood plywoods from just $\frac{1}{32}$ to $\frac{1}{2}$ inch and thicker are available. At right is a piece of MDF (medium-density fiberboard), which is good for painted projects.

1–3. Acrylic sheet plastics are available in clear, translucent, solid colors, and mirrored types. Corian (shown on the right) is one of various hard surface materials that cut extremely well with the scroll saw.

1–4. Thin sheet aluminum painted black. Thin plywood can be painted to look exactly the same as painted metal.

1–5. A special patina finish has been applied to this thin plywood to make it look like aged metal.

SCROLL SAWS

The majority of the projects can be made with any working scroll saw that will carry 5-inch plain-end blades (**1–6** and **1–7**). Sawing thick wood, such as when making several of the boxes in Chapter 9, will require a saw with more than the average thickness-cutting capacity. Making a very long name sign like the design in Chapter 10 may exceed the throat capacity of some machines. These are the only two situations that may create some cutting restrictions due to scroll saw capacity limitations.

1–6. A popular bench-top scroll saw with a 20-inch throat capacity.

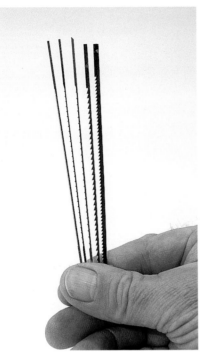

1–7. A variety of scroll saw blades. As a rule, use smaller blades for thin stock, tight turns, and small spaces. Use larger blades for thicker stock and larger curves.

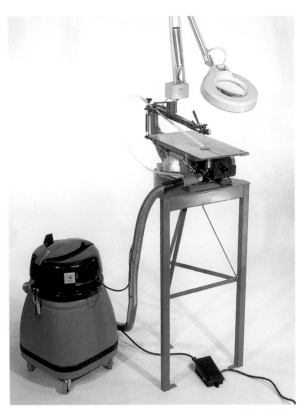

1–8. A floor-model saw equipped with a magnifying light and a shop vacuum system designed to extract fine dust from above the workpiece and from under the table.

1–9. A practical setup that collects airborne scroll-sawing dust and also works well for sanding, routing, and other dust-generating jobs. At right is a square household fan with a furnace filter taped to it. To the left, a small second fan to help move the air.

SAFETY TECHNIQUES

Always read the manufacturer's instructions and heed its warnings when using any product—especially those specifically related to scroll saws and other power-driven tools and those used for finishing. Always wear eye protection and utilize all safety provisions of the scroll saw. One of the most overlooked shop hazards is a dusty environment. Using adequate dust protection cannot be overemphasized since many very fine dust particles are generated with the scroll saw as well as during sanding and routing operations (**1–8** and **1–9**). A dust mask, while helpful, only catches larger particles. It is the invisible, micro-fine, airborne dust particles that must be dealt with and avoided. Hearing protection is also recommended when working around elevated noise levels. Dress safely (tuck in cuffs and sleeves and do not wear jewelry), maintain a clean working environment, and always be alert and free of mental or physical distractions when working in the shop.

GENERAL TECHNIQUES

Sizing Patterns

On a number of patterns in the following chapters are notes that state "Full-Size Pattern" or "Enlarge Pattern 'X' Percent." These directions are not always intended to be followed explicitly. By and large, they are merely suggestions for a practical size. In fact, sizing patterns to satisfy individual circumstances or needs is strongly encouraged. One practical example is to size the pattern to the size of stock that is available. That is, if the material is slightly smaller than the suggested size, it might be economically prudent to reduce the pattern size accordingly. Conversely, if the material available is slightly larger, it may be advantageous to enlarge the pattern size slightly rather than waste that extra material.

The proportional scale (**1–10** and **1–11**) is an inexpensive accessory scroll-sawers and artists use to determine the percentage to set the copy machine to obtain precisely the size pattern they want. Proportional scales are available at art supply shops and via mail order. They consist of two circular discs with numerical scales that rotate about a common center. Using the proportional

scale is simply a matter of matching up the numbers as shown in **1–11**. Match the number indicating the size of the pattern to the number indicating the size you want the pattern to be. The percentage to set the copy machine automatically appears in a "window" on the scale.

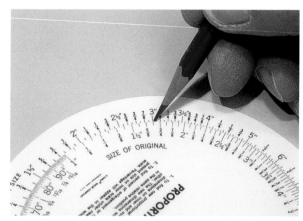

1–11. Simply rotate the scale to match up marks indicating the size of the given copy to the mark indicating the new copy size desired, as shown. Then read the percentage given in the proportional scale's window.

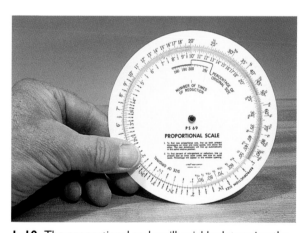

1–10. The proportional scale will quickly determine the exact percentage of enlargement or reduction when using the photocopy machine.

Applying Patterns to the Project Material

Today, the standard practice is to glue a photocopy of the pattern directly to the surface of the workpiece with a temporary bonding spray adhesive (**1–12**). The saw cuts through both the pattern and the workpiece. When sawing is completed, the pattern should remove almost effortlessly unless too much or the wrong kind of adhesive was applied. In such cases, it will be necessary to soften the adhesive with a solvent (turpentine or lacquer, depending upon the adhesive brand) to remove the pattern.

Preparing the Scroll Saw

Ensure that the correct blade is installed. Refer to the *New Scroll Saw Handbook* for a complete discussion of which blades to use for every possible scroll-sawing situation. Tension the blade and

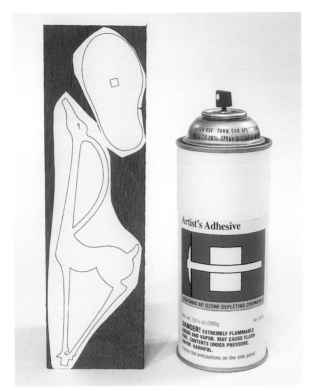

1–13. Using a protractor to set the table perfectly square or to a specific angle for bevel-sawing. This above-the-table technique is easier to read and more accurate than using the saw's scale normally located under the table, which is usually inaccurate.

1–12. Adhere a photocopy of the pattern directly to the workpiece. Use a temporary bonding type of spray adhesive applied very lightly to the back of the pattern copy only.

adjust the hold-down. Many photos show sawing with the blade guards and hold-downs removed. This is in part to make the illustration clearer, but also because the photos were taken on machines used by professional scroll-sawers who usually remove these devices because they limit their techniques for many jobs. Beginners and youngsters, however, should use all safety devices until an appropriate level of confidence and skill is attained through sufficient sawing experience.

Adjusting the Saw Table

For most sawing jobs, the table should be adjusted so it is perfectly square to the blade (**1–13**). Serious cutting defects will occur if cuts are made with the table tilted when it should be perfectly square. Close to square is not good enough, especially when stack sawing and precision sawing of thick material.

Stack-Sawing

Stack-sawing is the practice of sawing two or more layers of material at the same time. The advantages of this technique are twofold: First, it saves time. Second, every sawn piece from the stack will be identical. That is, of course, provided the cuts are made with the saw table adjusted perfectly square to the blade. If the table happens to be set so it is at an angle to the blade, the bottom layer of the stack will be cut to a different size than the top or pattern layer.

Holding layers together so they do not shift during stack-sawing is also essential. This can be accomplished in many different ways: Nails, tape, and glue are the methods most commonly used. It is important that the pieces be held tightly to each other without gaps between layers. Gaps may cause tearout or chipping of the cut edges between the layers.

Sometimes, in fact, bottom tear-out or feathering can be prevented by using a scrap layer (backer) under the workpiece. When using a scrap backer, the work must be prepared as if stack-sawing.

The recommended practice for preparing wood materials of any thickness for stack-sawing is nailing the layers together. Driving nails or brads into the waste or scrap areas is quick and easy. *Tip:* When nailing very thin materials together for stack-sawing, drive the nails while holding the pieces over a flat steel surface as shown in **1–14**. The nail points will peen (flatten) and firmly grip the thinnest of bottom layers and the nails will not scratch the scroll saw table. Certain plastics and some thin metals that cannot be nailed together easily are best held together with wraps of tape or spots of glue.

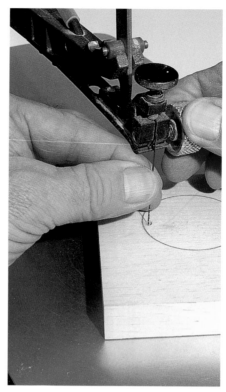

1–15. Threading the blade through a hole drilled in the waste to make an inside cut such as an opening for a clock insert.

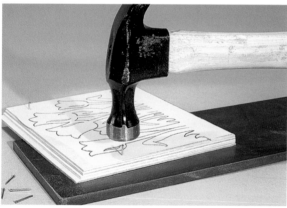

1–14. Driving brads through several layers of very thin plywood for stack-sawing. When done over a steel plate as shown, the nail points peen so they will hold the bottom layer secure and not scratch the saw table during cutting.

Making Inside Cutouts

Inside cutouts (**1–15**) are made by drilling a suitably sized hole into the waste area and threading the blade through the hole before attaching the blade into the blade clamps. Smaller openings require smaller holes and smaller blades.

Sanding

With proper sawing techniques, the resulting sawn edges produced with a scroll saw should, in almost every situation, be extremely smooth; so smooth, in fact, the surfaces appear almost as if polished. In wood, as a rule, the sawn surfaces should not require any sanding other than a "light touch" to soften sharp edges or remove minor feathering, which can occur on the exit or bottom edge of the cut. Bottom-side feathering can be reduced or totally eliminated by using blades with reverse lower teeth (**1–16**). *Tip:* Sometimes certain woods such as cherry will have a tendency to leave a burn along the sawn edges. In such cases, simply cover the cutting line with clear or colored packaging tape. Some ingredients of the tape lubricate and cool the cutting action and prevent burning or charred cuts (**1–17**). The results are amazing!

1–16. Using a flutter wheel removes feathering, softens sharp corners, and smooths routed edges as shown.

1–17. This photo clearly shows the dramatic effect plastic packaging tape has in alleviating burning tendencies when sawing solid cherry or other difficult-to-cut materials. A worn blade was used throughout the cut, in a left-to-right feed direction. Notice how the finish quality improved in the central area where the surface is covered with the packaging tape.

QUICK & HANDY PROJECTS

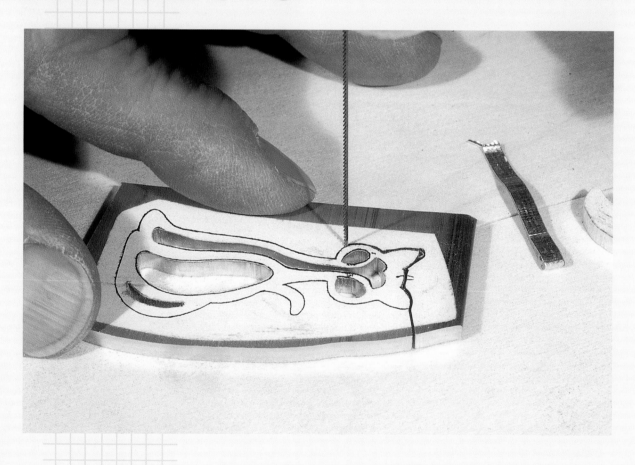

This chapter includes a number of unusual small projects and useful items for the home and office. Most can be made in a short period of time, often using scraps from other projects. Many items can also be cut from a variety of materials other than wood. To obtain information about performing unfamiliar cutting or finishing techniques, refer to Chapter 1 and/or to the *New Scroll Saw Handbook*.

SCROLL TOPS

These scroll tops (**2–1** and **2–2**) are made from a piece of ¼-inch-thick plywood 3 × 3 inches and a 2½-inch length of ¼-inch-diameter hardwood dowel. Cut out as per the pattern. The fretted openings make interesting designs as the top spins. Painting the sawn edges gives a dramatic look to the spinning top. The dowel can be shaped with a file as desired while chucked and rotating in a drill press. The drill press also can be used for assembly to glue the disc perfectly square to the dowel.

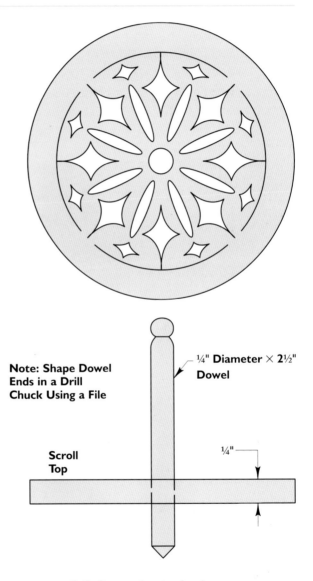

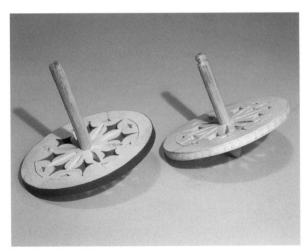

2–1. Scroll tops, painted on left, unfinished at right.

Note: Shape Dowel Ends in a Drill Chuck Using a File

¼" **Diameter × 2½" Dowel**

Scroll Top

¼"

2–2. Pattern drawing for the top.

WORKSHOP CALIPERS

Workshop calipers (**2–3** and **2–4**) are made from two pieces of serviceable plywood, metal, or plastic material ¹⁄₁₆ to ⅛ inch in thickness and 2 inches wide × 6½ inches long. Stack-saw the two pieces. Glue the round head of a ¼ × ½-inch machine bolt to one leg and assemble the pieces with a wing nut and lock washer over a fender washer on the opposite side.

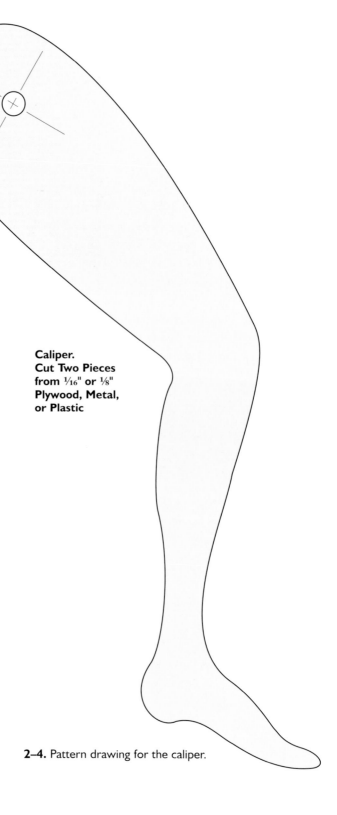

**Caliper.
Cut Two Pieces
from ¹⁄₁₆" or ⅛"
Plywood, Metal,
or Plastic**

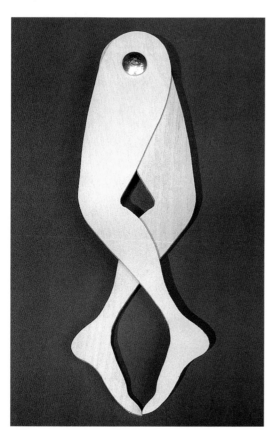

2–3. This caliper, based on a century-old design, is a fun project to make and have around any shop.

2–4. Pattern drawing for the caliper.

SMALL PAPER CLIPS/BOOKMARKS

These items (**2–5** and **2–6**) are cut from ⅟₃₂-inch Baltic-birch plywood 2 inches wide × 2¼ inches long. Stack-sawing various quantities is recommended because you'll want more than just one.

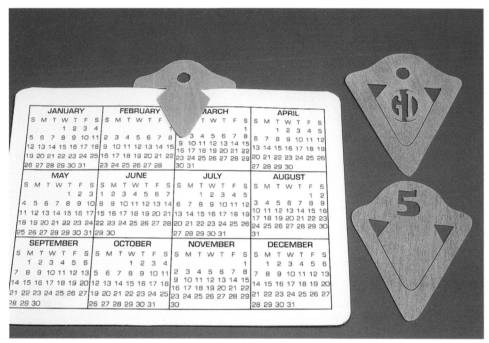

2–5. Wooden paper clips that can also be used as bookmarks. Notice that they can be personalized with pierced-cut initials, numbers, or other small designs.

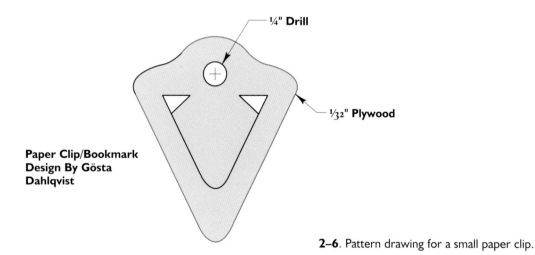

¼" **Drill**

⅟₃₂" **Plywood**

Paper Clip/Bookmark Design By Gösta Dahlqvist

2–6. Pattern drawing for a small paper clip.

LARGE PAPER CLIPS

These large paper clips (**2–7** and **2–8**) are made of ¹⁄₁₆-inch-thick Baltic-birch plywood. The clip itself is 2½ inches wide and 6 inches long, or 7 inches long for the standing version, which has an extra tab that fits a slot cut into a solid-wood base (1 × 2½ × 3¼ inches).

STANDING GAZELLE

The standing gazelle (**2–7** and **2–8**) requires two pieces of ¼-inch- thick solid hardwood. One piece is 3 × 9 inches, and the other 2⅛ × 4⅛ inches.

LETTER OPENERS

The letter openers shown in **2–7** and **2–9** are made from any serviceable ³⁄₁₆-inch-thick solid hardwood. Sizes range from 1⅛ to 2 inches in width and 7½ to 8½ inches in length. File and sand to shape edges as necessary. To personalize, enlarge, or reduce any appropriate initial pattern to fit, see page 164 or refer to *Alphabets & Numbers* by Patrick Spielman and Sherri Valitchka, Sterling Publishing Company.

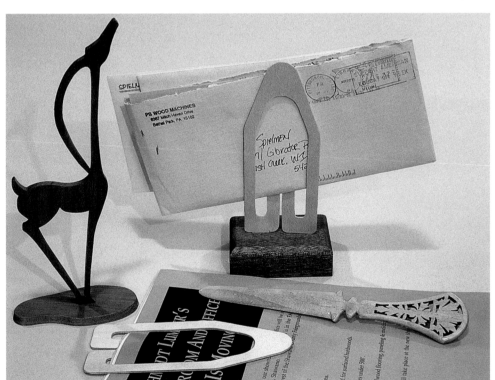

2–7. Mahogany gazelle, large Baltic birch paper clip/message holder, and solid-maple letter opener.

2–8. Pattern drawings for a large paper clip and a standing gazelle.

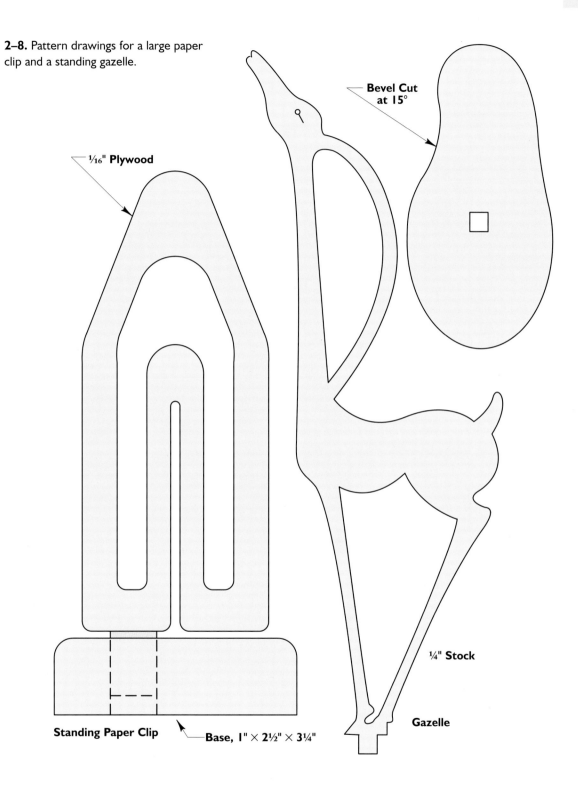

1/16" Plywood

Bevel Cut
at 15°

1/4" Stock

Gazelle

Standing Paper Clip

Base, 1" × 2½" × 3¼"

2–9. Patterns for letter openers.

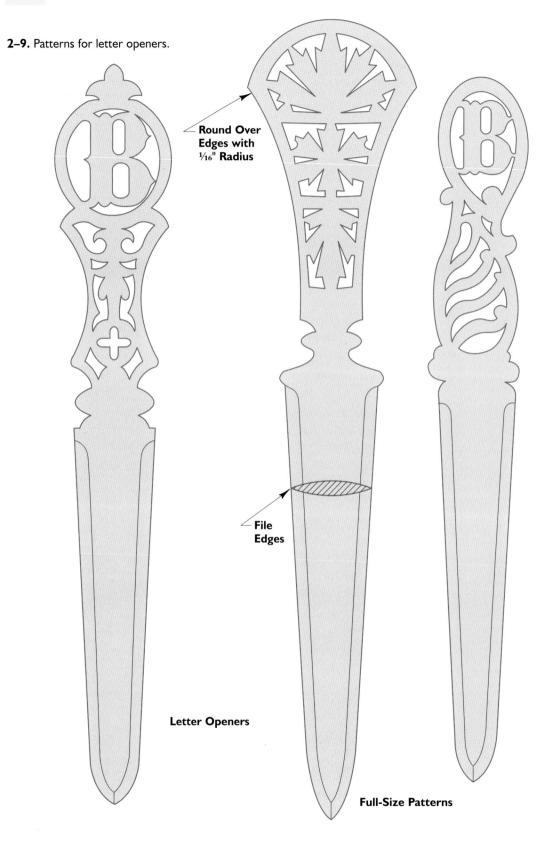

**Round Over
Edges with
¹⁄₁₆" Radius**

**File
Edges**

Letter Openers

Full-Size Patterns

KEY CHAINS

The key chains shown in **2–10** and **2–11** are scroll-sawn and glue-laminated together (face to face) in such a way that the area around the design appears to be cut away. Use any of the designs suggested or create your own using appropriate symbols or personalized initials as discussed for the following project. Begin with suitable hardwood of your choice that's ⅜ to ½ inch thick, 2 inches wide, and 2 or 2¼ inches long. Cut a thin slice (⅛ inch or less) off the back as shown in **2–11**. Then cut the design and face piece from the remaining, thicker piece. Glue the face to the backer. Curve the surfaces and edge as desired with a sander and apply a finish of your choice.

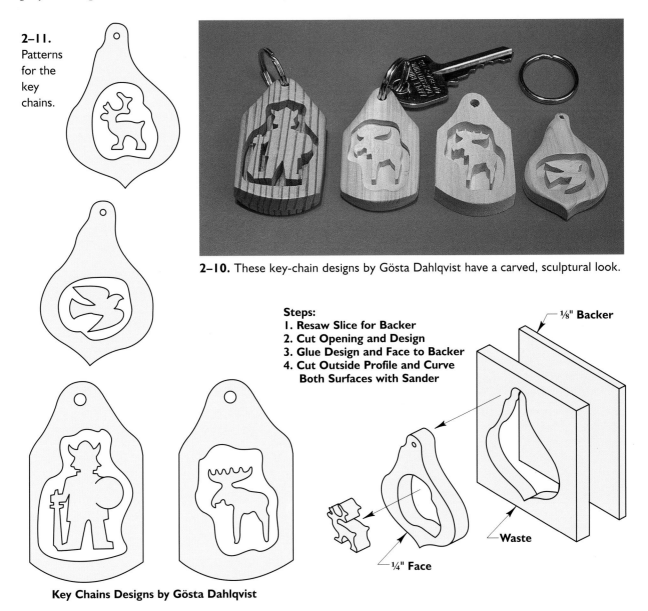

2–11. Patterns for the key chains.

2–10. These key-chain designs by Gösta Dahlqvist have a carved, sculptural look.

Steps:
1. Resaw Slice for Backer
2. Cut Opening and Design
3. Glue Design and Face to Backer
4. Cut Outside Profile and Curve Both Surfaces with Sander

⅛" **Backer**

Waste

¼" **Face**

Key Chains Designs by Gösta Dahlqvist

SMALL DESIGNS FOR JEWELRY, ETC.

Small pieces of scrap hardwood, various metals, and plastics can be used to make jewelry (**2–12** to **2-14**). Some of the less complex designs can be used as inlays, and most of the designs shown in **2–13** and **2–14** can be used as overlays on small boxes, etc.

Use a copy machine to enlarge or reduce the patterns as desired for various applications. Illus. **2–15** and **2–16** show the scroll-sawing of brass. Silver sheet makes beautiful pendants that can also be cut on the scroll saw, as shown in **2–17** and **2–18**.

2–12. Small scroll-sawn cutouts and jewelry made from a variety of materials, including brass, copper, silver, and Corian.

2–13. Patterns for small jewelry designs.

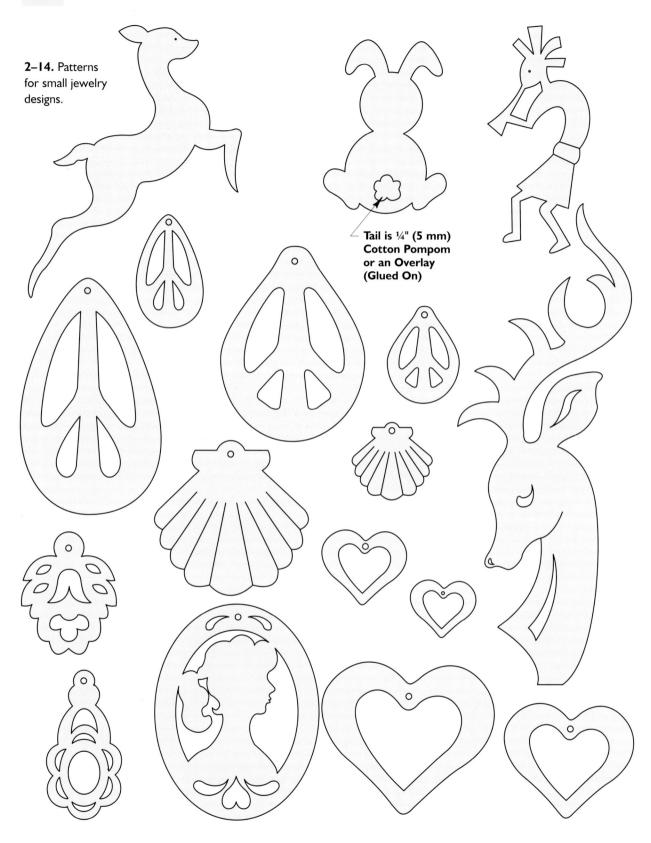

2–14. Patterns for small jewelry designs.

Tail is ¼" (5 mm) Cotton Pompom or an Overlay (Glued On)

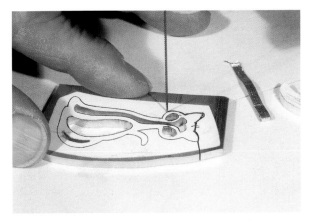

2–15. Using a metal-cutting blade to cut ⅛-inch brass.

2–16. The edge is relatively smooth on this piece of brass sawn while supported on a waste wood backer.

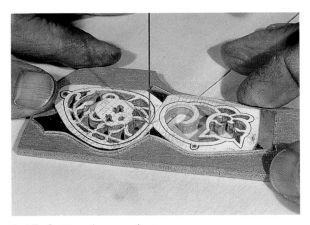

2–17. Cutting silver pendants.

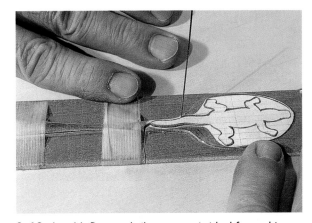

2–18. An old, flattened silver spoon is ideal for making scroll-sawn jewelry.

UNICORN SCULPTURE

The unicorn sculpture makes a good paperweight or shelf decoration. The unicorn shown in **2–19** is made of Corian, but other materials of choice can be used and the pattern sized as desired. The unicorn shown in **2–20** is cut from ½ × 4 × 5½-inch Corian and is glued to a ½ x 2 × 4-inch base. If using Corian, glue the assembly with instant or epoxy glue.

ACRYLIC ACROBAT SCULPTURE

To make the acrylic acrobat sculpture featured in **2–19** and **2–21**, use ⅛- or ¼-inch-thick 5 × 7-inch material and cut a ⅜-inch-deep groove to fit into a solid-wood ¾ × 1¾ × 6¼-inch base.

"WINGS" SCULPTURE

The sculpture shown in **2–19** is made of unfinished ⅛-inch birch plywood; however, as with many projects, it could also be cut from metal or plastic. Cut it to the pattern size as given in **2-22**, enlarge it 111 percent to duplicate the one made by the author, or size the pattern to any size you desire. The base is made from ¾-inch-thick material with beveled edges cut on the scroll saw.

2–19. Left: Unicorn cut from ½-inch Corian. Center: acrobat cut from ⅛-inch clear acrylic plastic. Right: "Wings" cut from ⅛-inch Baltic birch plywood. All designs by Bev Carmody.

2–20. Pattern for the unicorn.

½"
← **Thick**

← **Base, ½" × 2" × 4"**

Unicorn
Design By Bev Carmody

2–21. Pattern for the acrobat.

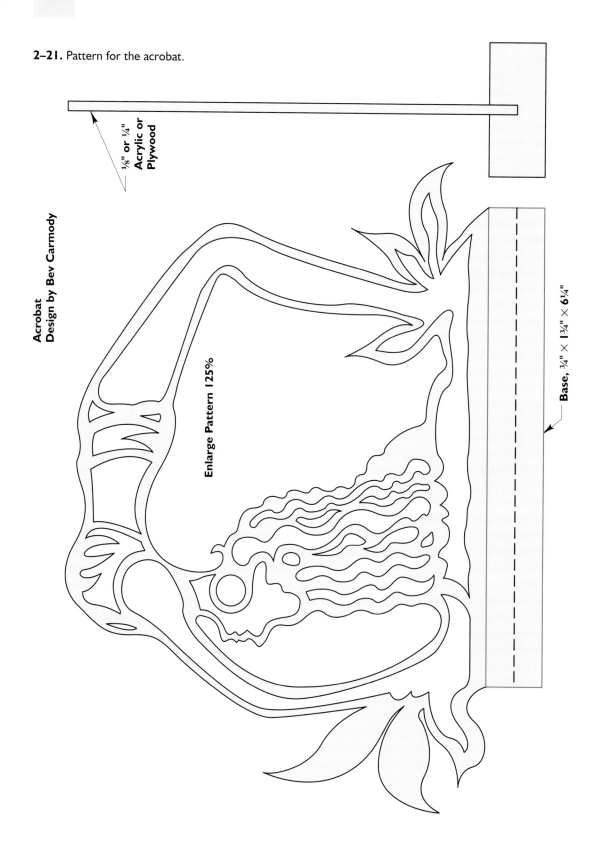

1/8" or 1/4"
Acrylic or Plywood

Acrobat
Design by Bev Carmody

Enlarge Pattern 125%

Base, 3/4" × 1 3/4" × 6 1/4"

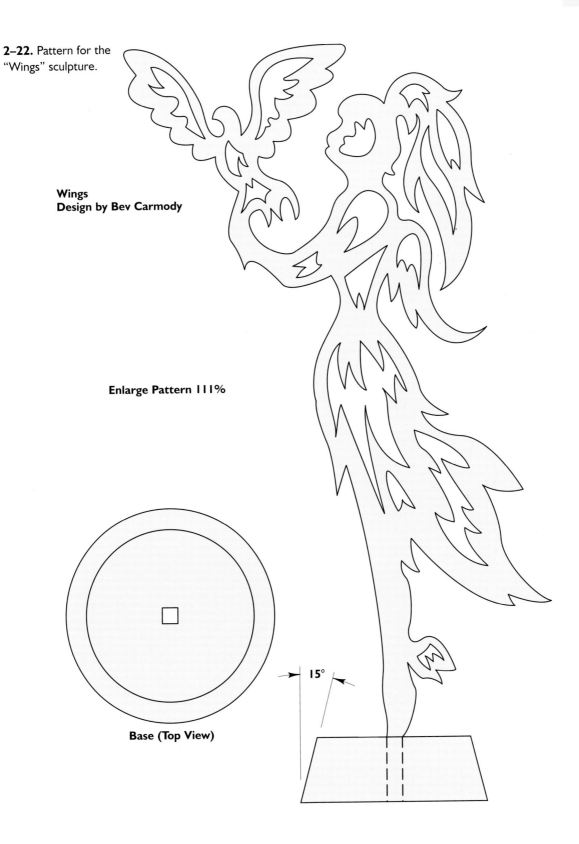

2–22. Pattern for the "Wings" sculpture.

**Wings
Design by Bev Carmody**

Enlarge Pattern 111%

Base (Top View)

15°

KOKOPELLI SCULPTURE

The kokopelli sculpture (**2–23** and **2–24**) is designed to be made of ½-inch-thick Corian; however, a hardwood of your choice or a spray-painted stone-textured finish also will look very nice. Two pieces of stock are required: one piece 3½ × 6½ inches and another 1⅝ × 4⅛ inches. Simply cut out the patterns and assemble them. The base is bevel-sawn at 15 degrees. Use epoxy or instant glue if Corian is used.

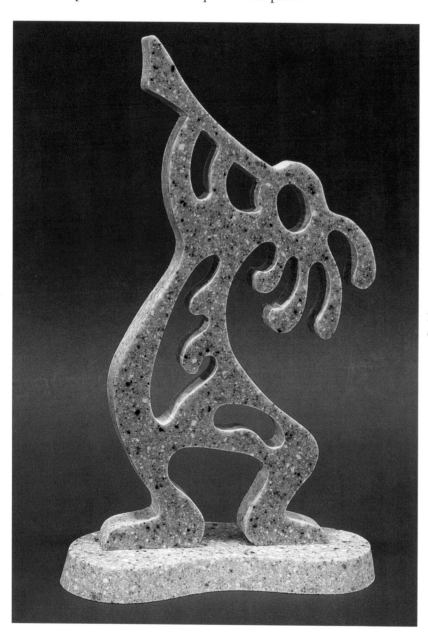

2–23. Kokopelli sculpture shown cut from ½-inch-thick Corian.

2–24. Pattern for the Kokopelli.

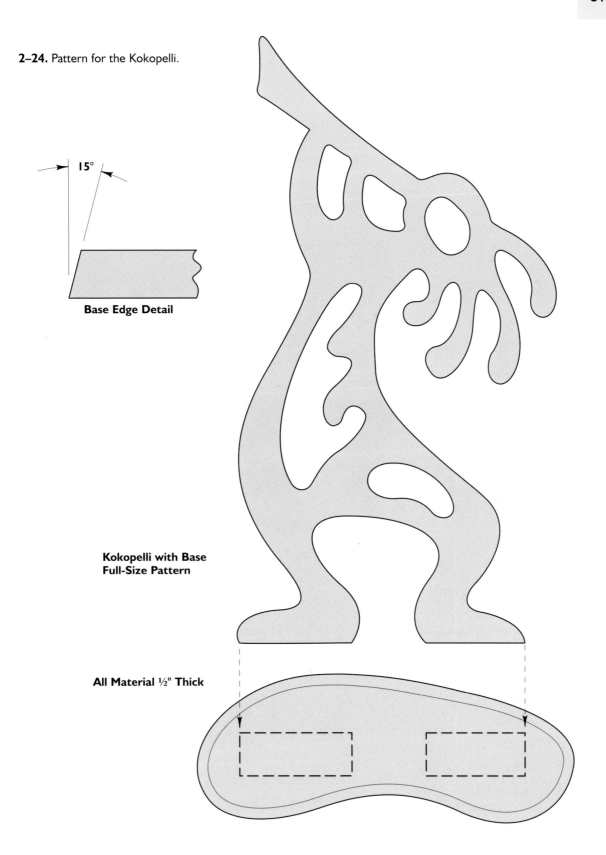

15°

Base Edge Detail

**Kokopelli with Base
Full-Size Pattern**

All Material ½" Thick

EYE SCULPTURE

The eye sculpture (**2–25** and **2–26**) is another project intended to be a paperweight or just a shelf decoration cut from ½-inch Corian. However, any material of choice can be used. Use the pattern size as given in **2–26** or enlarge it 125 percent.

DANCER

This project (**2–25** and **2–26**) can also be made from a variety of materials ⅛ inch thick or thicker. Use the pattern size as given or enlarge it as desired. Cut a base from ½-inch-thick material to a 2½-inch diameter with a square or optional 15-degree beveled edge.

2–25. Corian eye sculpture and a trio of dancers. Left: cut from wood and with a weathered metal/patina finish. Center: Black painted wood. Right: Smoked acrylic plastic with a Corian base.

2–26. Patterns for the dancer and eye sculpture.

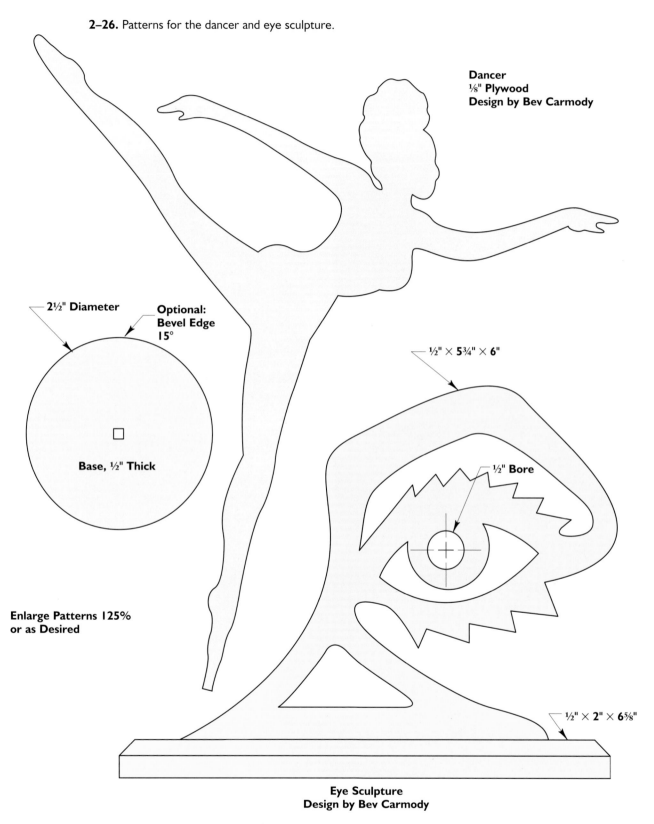

Dancer
⅛" Plywood
Design by Bev Carmody

2½" Diameter

Optional:
Bevel Edge
15°

½" × 5¾" × 6"

Base, ½" Thick

½" Bore

Enlarge Patterns 125%
or as Desired

½" × 2" × 6⅝"

Eye Sculpture
Design by Bev Carmody

FLUORESCENT ALIEN

To make the alien shown in **2–27** to **2–30**, enlarge the patterns to the desired size. Then cut the shape, round over the sawn edges (**2–28**), and paint it a greenish fluorescent color. Use the entire project as a decoration for a child's room, as a yard ornament, or attach the head alone to a stake to use as a driveway marker (**2–29**).

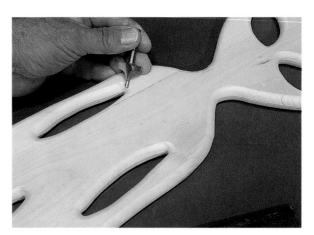

2–28. Rounding over the edges using a bit with a small integral pilot that gets into tight corners.

2–27. Fluorescent alien cutout.

2–29. The alien head as a driveway marker. The eyes can be sawn from plastic reflectors and screwed to the face.

2–30. Patterns for alien.

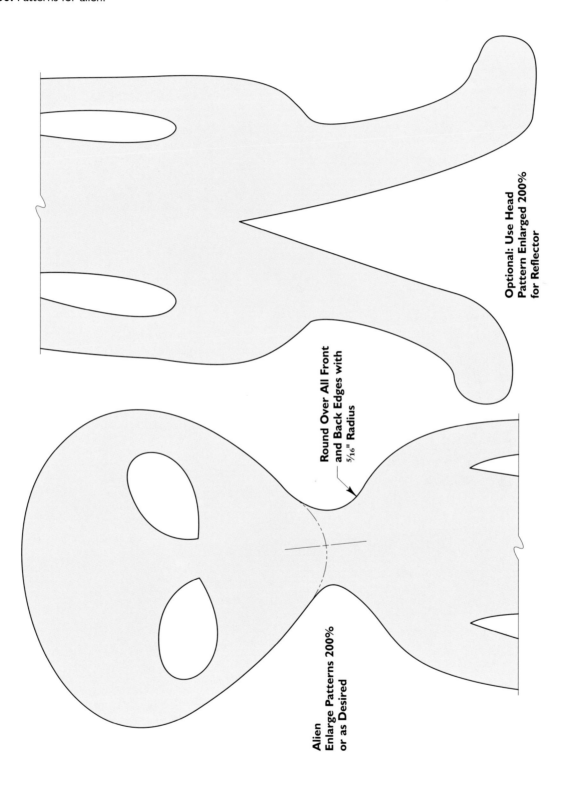

Optional: Use Head Pattern Enlarged 200% for Reflector

Round Over All Front and Back Edges with 5/16" Radius

Alien
Enlarge Patterns 200% or as Desired

DIMENSIONAL BUTTERFLIES

These delicate, decorative, and eye-catching projects (**2–31** to **2–33**) are made from thin (¹⁄₃₂- or ¹⁄₁₆-inch-thick) plywoods or sawn from thin, stiff cardboard. They are best produced in various quantities by stack-sawing many layers of material all at the same time. If sawing just a few, stack-saw the inside openings and the outside profile shapes. Then separate the stack into two stacks and saw each stack differently as per the patterns to make the slots for the halved joints. *Tip*: Dip-finish the project in various colors or leave it natural.

2–32. These delicate, dimensional butterflies are sawn from layers of thin plywood or stiff cardboard.

2–31. Patterns for the butterflies.

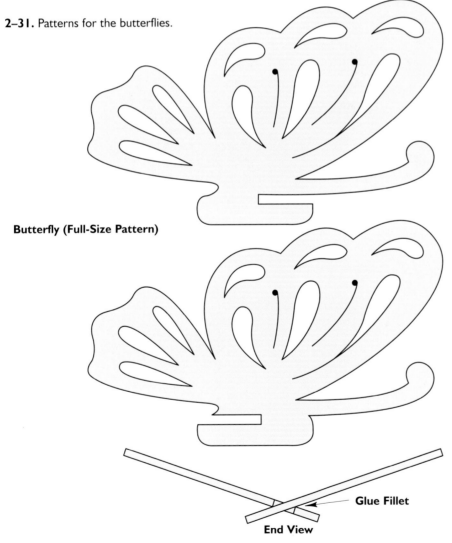

Butterfly (Full-Size Pattern)

Glue Fillet

End View

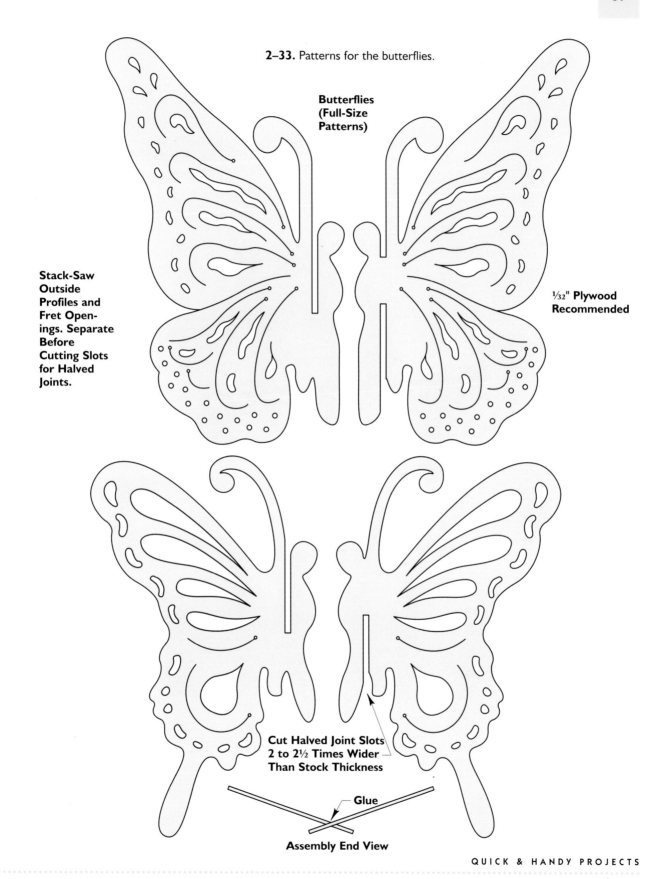

2–33. Patterns for the butterflies.

**Butterflies
(Full-Size
Patterns)**

**Stack-Saw
Outside
Profiles and
Fret Open-
ings. Separate
Before
Cutting Slots
for Halved
Joints.**

**¹⁄₃₂" Plywood
Recommended**

**Cut Halved Joint Slots
2 to 2½ Times Wider
Than Stock Thickness**

Glue

Assembly End View

WALKING FISH

This fun project (**2–34** and **2–35**) is best made from ⅜- or ½-inch-thick stock. Cut two side fins. Fin and leg placement locations are indicated by dashed lines on the pattern. Use brightly colored acrylic paints and apply without restrictions. Have fun and allow your creativity to run wild while painting this one-of-a-kind piece of art.

2–34. Walking fish, a whimsical project designed and created by R. Stephan Toman.

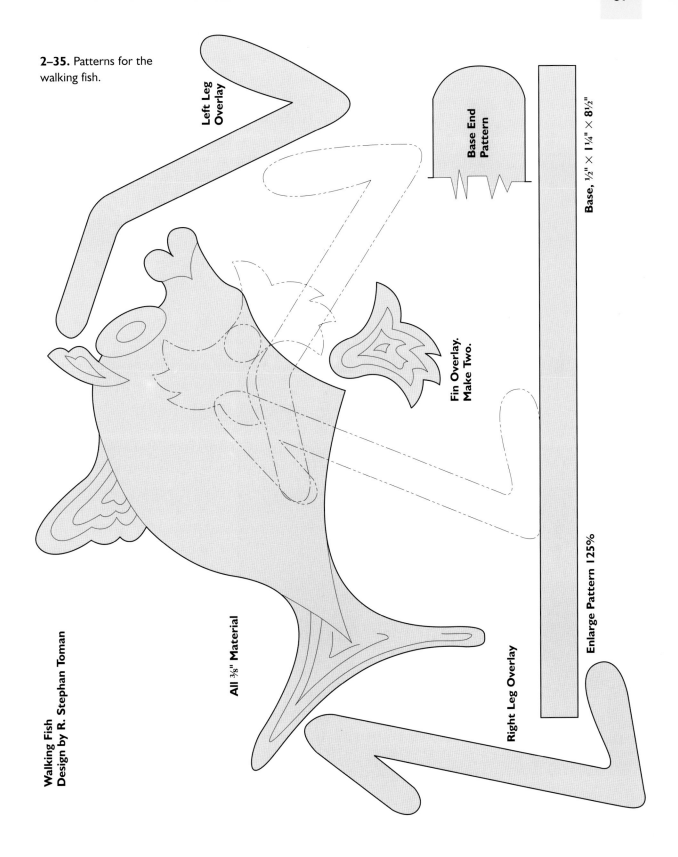

2–35. Patterns for the walking fish.

Left Leg Overlay

Base End Pattern

Base, ½" × 1¼" × 8½"

Fin Overlay. Make Two.

Enlarge Pattern 125%

Right Leg Overlay

All ⅜" Material

Walking Fish
Design by R. Stephan Toman

BODIE ISLAND HOUSE

This standing project (**2–36** and **2–37**) can be made any size. Use ¼- to ½-inch stock with a ¾-inch-thick base. Assemble with a tab-and-slot construction that is cut to fit. Leave unfinished or finish to suit.

2–36. Bodie Island lighthouse.

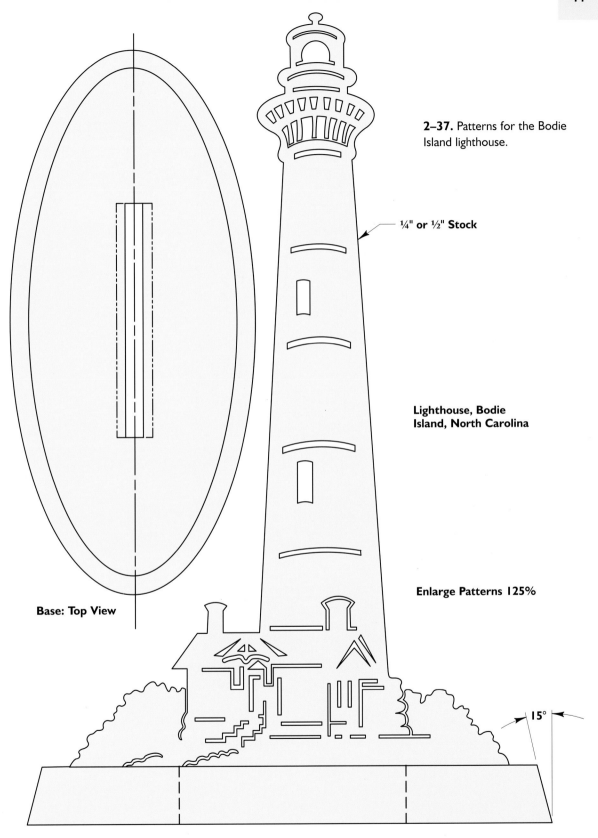

2–37. Patterns for the Bodie Island lighthouse.

¼" or ½" Stock

Lighthouse, Bodie
Island, North Carolina

Enlarge Patterns 125%

Base: Top View

15°

EIFFEL TOWER

This project (**2–38** to **2–40**) is designed to be made from ⅛-inch-thick plywood. *Important*: Check the actual thickness of your material to be sure it matches the widths of the various slot openings of the enlarged pattern. Modify the pattern lines if necessary. The project assembles without glue and can be disassembled for flat storage or shipping. Leave it unfinished or apply a clear or pigmented finish as desired.

2–38. Patterns for the Eiffel Tower.

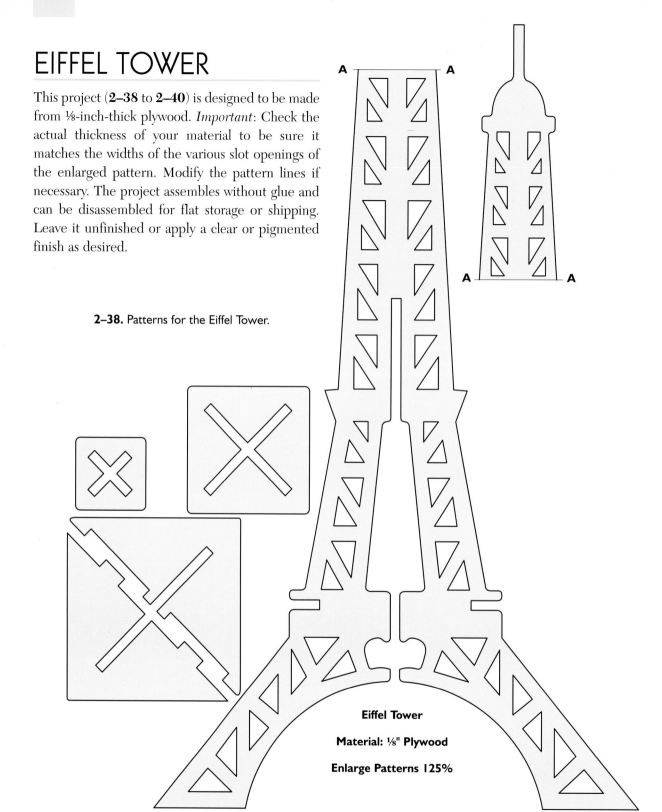

Eiffel Tower

Material: ⅛" Plywood

Enlarge Patterns 125%

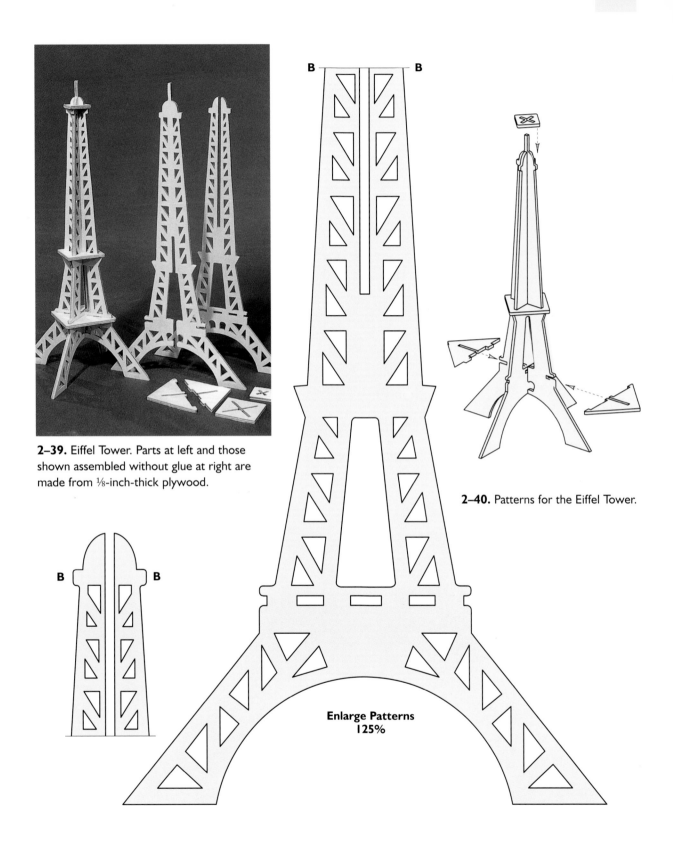

2–39. Eiffel Tower. Parts at left and those shown assembled without glue at right are made from ⅛-inch-thick plywood.

2–40. Patterns for the Eiffel Tower.

B   B

B   B

Enlarge Patterns 125%

HOLIDAY
ORNAMENTS

This chapter features over 60 project patterns that can be used to make a wide assortment of hanging ornaments and sun catchers for Valentine's Day, St. Patrick's Day, Easter, Halloween, and Christmas. To make quantities of any given design, stack multiple layers of the material together and cut them all at the same time. Plywoods from ⅟32 to ¼ inch thick are just one choice of many suitable materials to use. Solid woods ⅛ to ¼ inch thick are also recommended; however, for some designs, they may be too delicate and fragile. Explore the possibility of using other sheet materials including thin cardboards, acrylic plastics, and sheet metals such as brass, copper, and aluminum. All project designs involve basic scroll-sawing techniques, and all of the patterns are full-size and ready to use. Sizes, however, are easily modified (enlarged or reduced) with the use of a photocopy machine.

The finishing options for ornaments made of wood are many, with the specific choice up to the scroll-sawer. Thin plywoods look good without any finish at all. Thin solid woods can be dip-finished in Danish oil for an easy-to-apply natural finish. To color light woods, dip them in dye or color stains. Another good coloring technique is to spray-finish the wood first, *before* applying the pattern. In this case, leave the sawn edges unfinished for a nice contrast. You may also want to explore various special finishes that are sold in department stores and home centers. Products are available to make wood look like bright, shiny metal or aged and antique-looking. Be sure to test all finishes on scrap of the same material so you know the end results before starting.

The projects and patterns depicted in **3–1** to **3–5** do not have specific instructions.

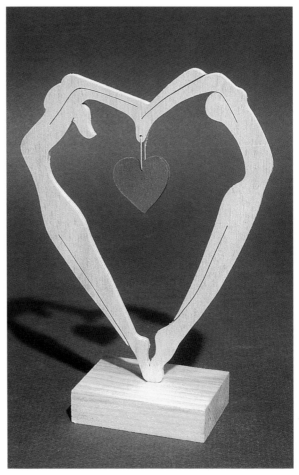

3–1. "Love" sculpture and some heart designs made of unfinished plywood.

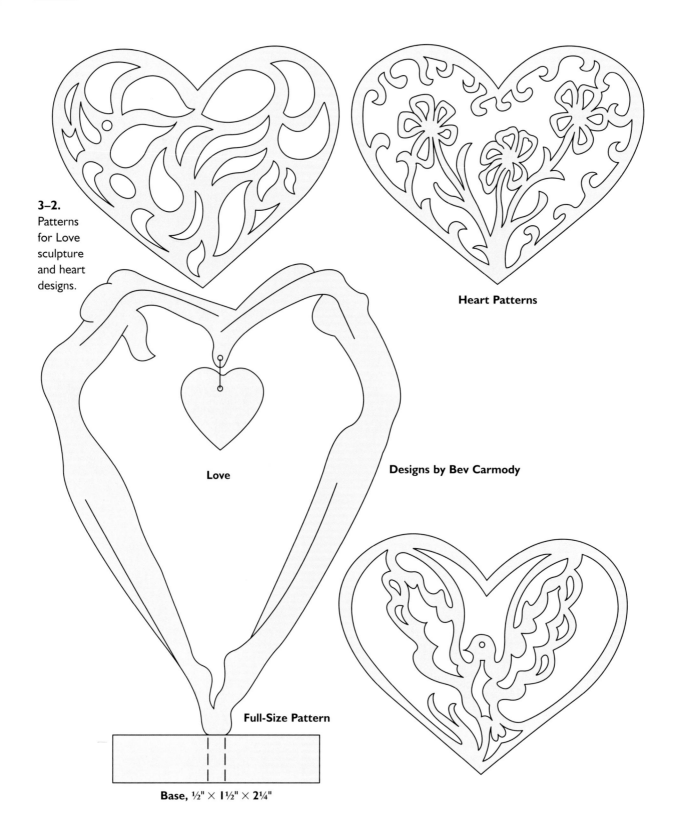

3–2.
Patterns for Love sculpture and heart designs.

Heart Patterns

Love

Designs by Bev Carmody

Full-Size Pattern

Base, ½" × 1½" × 2¼"

3–3. Patterns for the heart and shamrock designs.

**Heart
Design by Bragi
Baldursson**

**Lucky
Shamrocks**

**Cut at Thickness
of $1/32$" to $1/2$"**

Enlarge Patterns as Desired

**Heart
Designs by Brian Dahlen**

Enlarge Patterns 200%

Cut from $1/8$" Plywood

3–4. Pattern for alien bat.

Alien Bat
Design by Bev Carmody

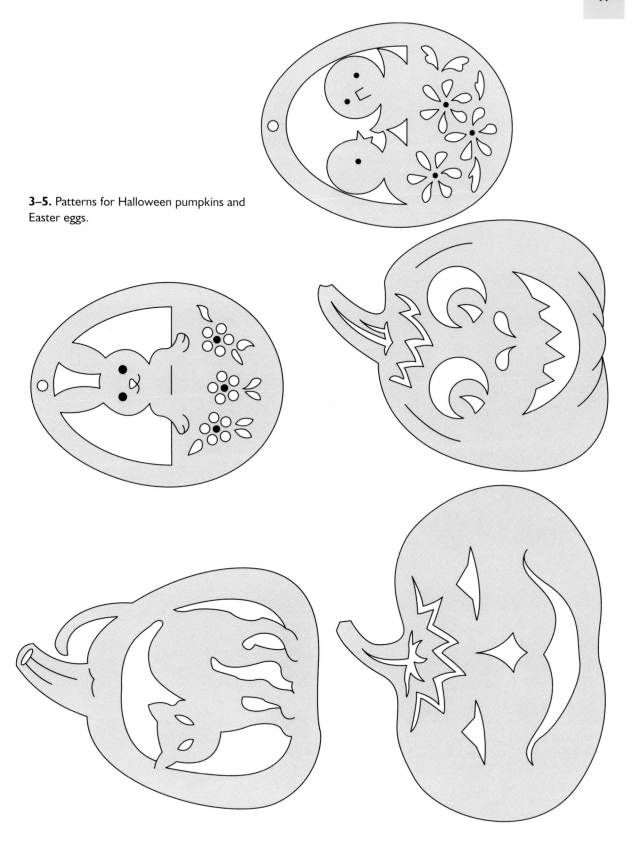

3–5. Patterns for Halloween pumpkins and Easter eggs.

STICK ORNAMENTS

Standard ¹⁄₁₆-inch-thick, solid-birch tongue depressors are a good choice of material for making these popular Scandinavian star-type ornaments (**3–6**). Four tongue depressors or pieces of plywood ¾ inch thick and six inches long are required for each ornament (**3–7**). Stack-saw them all at once as shown in **3–8**. Assemble them with glue (**3–9**) and finish them with color stains, fabric dye (**3–10**), or other finish of choice.

3–7. A variety of Scandinavian stick ornaments made from tongue depressors.

3–6. Three different kinds of ornaments: fretted, Scandinavian stick, and ornaments made with stack segmentation.

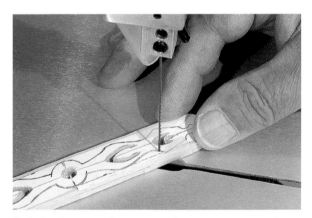

3–8. Stack-sawing four tongue depressors at once. A wrap of masking tape holds the stacked pad together.

3–9. A paper guide helps to position and space the pieces for gluing.

3–10. Dip-finishing the project in fabric dye available at the local grocery store. Tip: Heat water to a near boiling temperature before adding the dye. Also, dip the wood at near boiling temperature to achieve the best color brilliance. Allow the wood to dry and coat it with a satin spray polyurethane finish.

3–11. Patterns for the Scandinavian stick-ornament designs.

Full-Size Patterns

MISCELLANEOUS ORNAMENTS

Illus. **3–12** to **3–16** show patterns for miscellaneous ornaments with no specific instructions.

3–12. Pattern for peace dove.

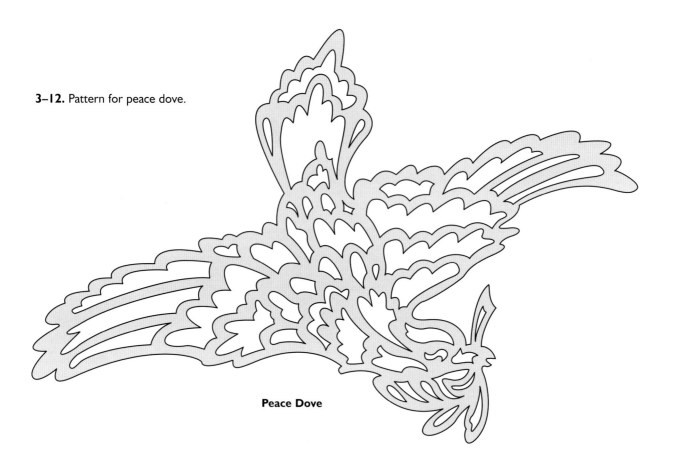

Peace Dove

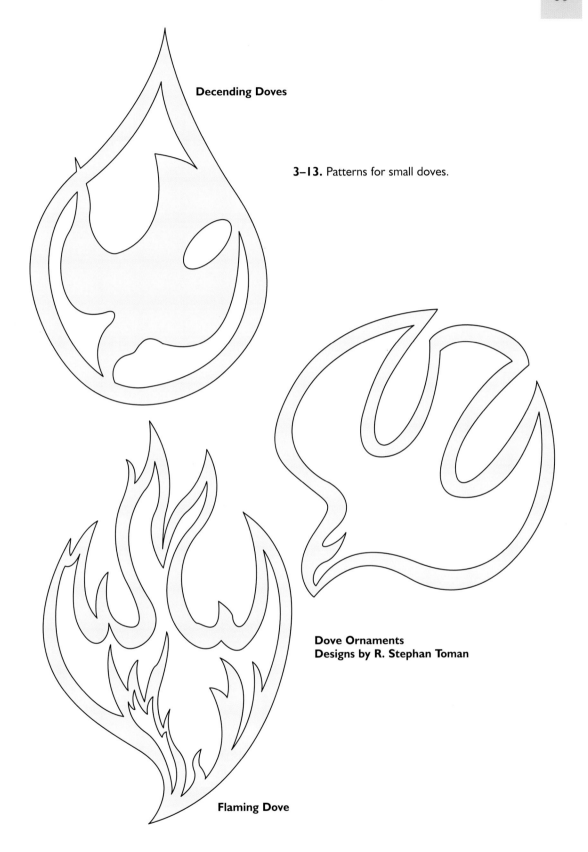

Decending Doves

3–13. Patterns for small doves.

**Dove Ornaments
Designs by R. Stephan Toman**

Flaming Dove

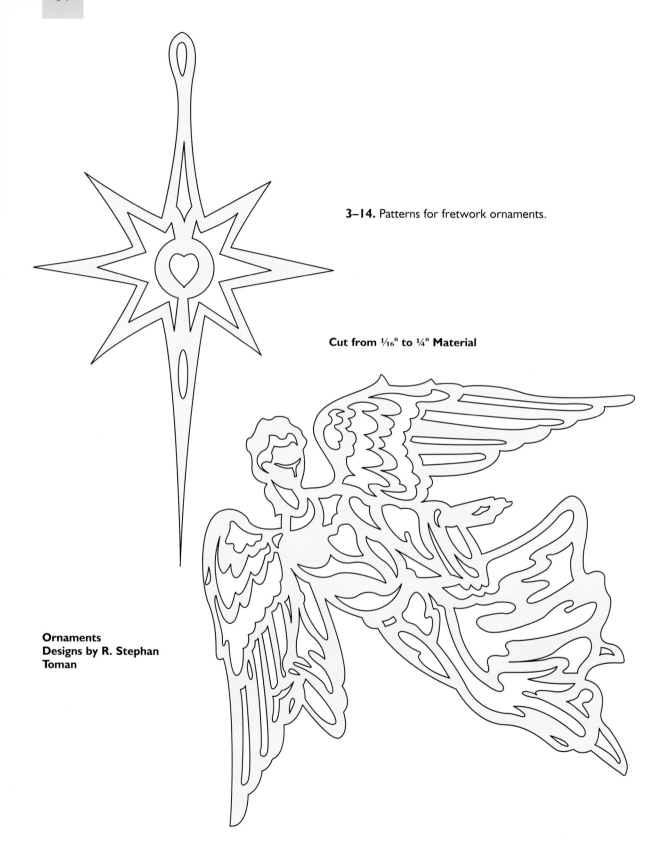

3–14. Patterns for fretwork ornaments.

Cut from ⅟₁₆" to ¼" Material

**Ornaments
Designs by R. Stephan
Toman**

3–15. Patterns for fretwork ornaments.

Cut from ⅟₃₂" to ¼" Thick Material

**Ornaments
Designs by Bev Carmody**

HOLIDAY ORNAMENTS

3–16. Patterns for angels made with fretwork and stack segmentation.

**Patterns Full
Size. Use
Material Up
to ¼" in
Thickness**

Fretwork Angels

Segmented Angel

STACKED SEGMENTED DOVE AND BELL ORNAMENTS

To make the bell ornaments (**3–17** to **3–19**), stack-saw two contrasting ¼ × 3 × 3-inch woods together. Ash and padauk were used for the projects shown in **3–17**. Cut the parts, interchange the pieces, and glue them together. *Tip*: Use gap-filling epoxy glue and glue with the project placed on a flat surface covered with wax paper. Sand the project flat and apply a natural finish. The dove and the bell patterns in **3–18** are made in the same way, but four or more different woods of your choice are used (**3–19**). The colors are provided by the natural woods themselves.

3–17. Left and lower: Stacked segmentation ornaments made of solid hardwoods along with some fretwork ornaments made of various materials.

3–18. Patterns for the dove and bell, which are made with stacked segmentation.

Grain Direction

Stacked Segmentation Ornaments

Full-Size Patterns
Use ⅛" to ¼" Thick Material

Grain Direction

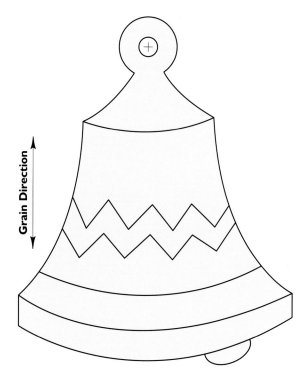

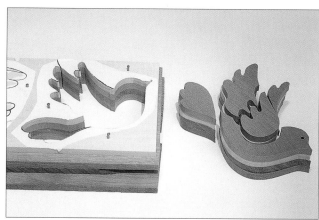

3–19. Four different woods are stack-sawn into parts. The parts are then interchanged, glued together (at the edges), sanded, and finally coated with a natural finish.

MISCELLANOUS ORNAMENTS

Illus. **3–20** to **3–24** show patterns for ornaments with no specific instructions.

3–20. Pattern for fretwork angels ornament.

Design by R. Stephan Toman

Fretwork Angels

Full-Size Pattern

3–21. Pattern for fretwork nativity ornament.

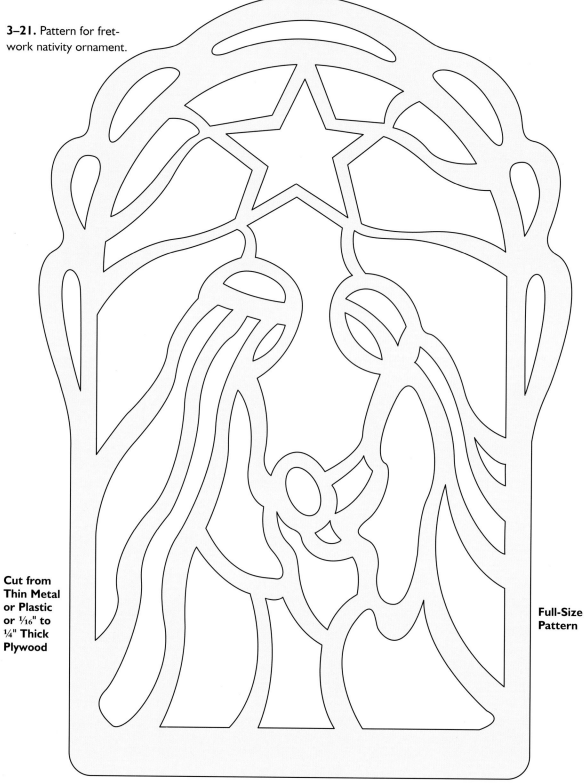

**Cut from
Thin Metal
or Plastic
or 1/16" to
1/4" Thick
Plywood**

**Full-Size
Pattern**

Fretwork Nativity

3–22. Patterns for jazz angels ornaments.

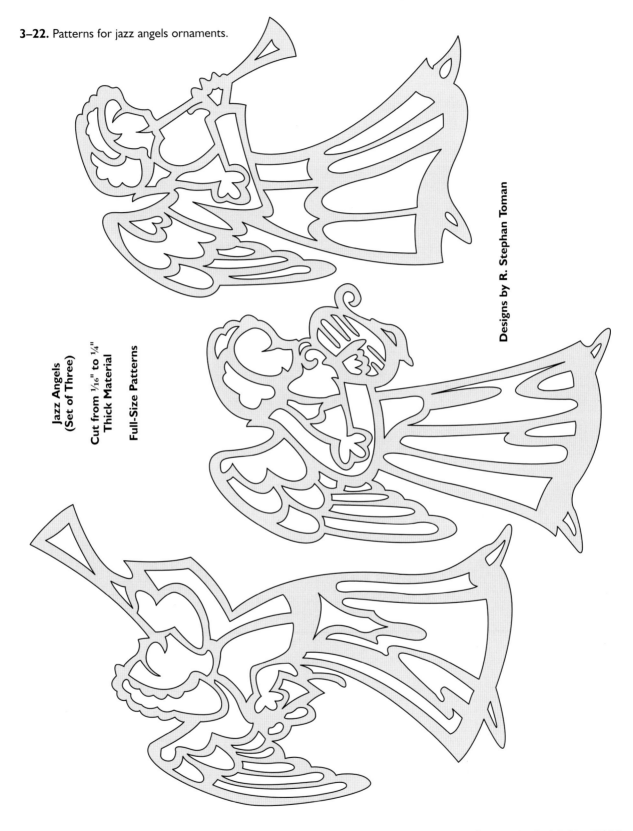

**Jazz Angels
(Set of Three)**

**Cut from $\frac{1}{16}$" to $\frac{1}{4}$"
Thick Material**

Full-Size Patterns

Designs by R. Stephan Toman

3–23. Pattern for Partridge in a
Pear Tree ornament.

**Partridge in a Pear Tree
Design by R. Stephan Toman**

3–24. Pattern for fretwork angel ornament.

Make from ⅛" to ¼" Plywood or Acrylic Plastic

**Angel
Design by
Bev Carmody**

FRETWORK OR FAUX STAINED-GLASS ANGELS

To create a stained-glass look (**3–25** to **3–27**), stack-saw two or more layers of ⅛ × 3 ⅝ × 6½-inch Baltic-birch plywood. Simulated stained glass is made by sandwiching a piece of plastic between two layers of the fretwork-sawn pieces. Color a piece of plastic film with permanent felt-tip markers or use glass stain obtained at craft stores.

Construction tips: Roughen the plastic surfaces with steel wool. This makes the colors more intense. Color the plastic while holding it over a photocopy of the pattern and fill in the appropriate spaces with the colors of your choice or duplicate the ones shown in the **3–25**. Stain or color both surfaces of the plastic. Trim the plastic to the outside shape of the angel. Leave the fretwork unfinished or spray it with a metallic coating. Glue the assembly together using model cement or instant glue.

3–26. Angel ornaments of unfinished Baltic-birch plywood. Designs by Paula Zinngrabe Wendland.

3–25. Faux stained-glass ornaments have transparent plastic colored with permanent felt-tip markers sandwiched between fret-sawn plywood.

3–27. Patterns for fretwork and simulated stained-glass angels.

Angel with Star

Full-Size Patterns

Angel with Wreath

Designs by Paula Zinngrabe Wendland

"THE TWELVE DAYS OF CHRISTMAS" ORNAMENT SET

This project (**3–28** to **3–31**), designed by R.S. Toman, depicts the lyrics to the traditional Christmas song.

3–28. "The Twelve Days of Christmas" ornament set sawn from ⅛-inch white translucent acrylic plastic.

3–29. Patterns for "A Partridge in a Pear Tree," "Two Turtle Doves," "Three French Hens," and "Four Calling Birds."

Twelve Days of Christmas

A Partridge in a Pear Tree

Two Turtle Doves

**Full-Size
Patterns**

Three French Hens

Four Calling Birds

3–30. Patterns for "Five Golden Rings," "Six Geese A-Laying," "Seven Swans A-Swimming," and "Eight Maids A-Milking."

Twelve Days of Christmas

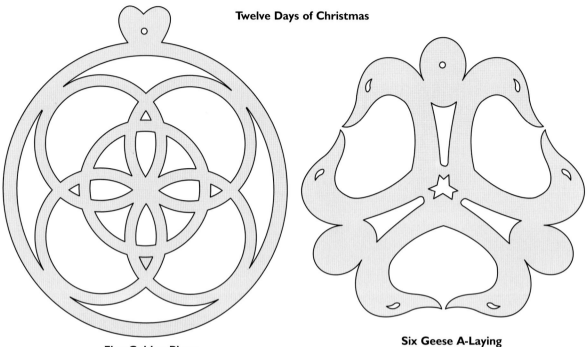

Five Golden Rings

Six Geese A-Laying

**Designs by R. Stephan
Toman
Full-Size Patterns**

Seven Swans A-Swimming

Eight Maids A-Milking

3–31. Patterns for "Nine Ladies Dancing," "Ten Lords A-Leaping," "Eleven Pipers Piping," and "Twelve Drummers Drumming."

Twelve Days of Christmas

Full-Size Patterns

Nine Ladies Dancing

Ten Lords A-Leaping

Eleven Pipers Piping

Twelve Drummers Drumming

OLD GERMAN CHRISTMAS SILHOUETTES

These delicate designs (**3–32** to **3–34**) are best cut from thin metal or high-quality Baltic-birch plywood. *Tips:* Aluminum house siding scraps found at construction sites can be scroll-sawn. Apply wax to the blade and sandwich the work between two pieces of scrap plywood. This will produce smooth, burr-free cuts. Spray-paint these projects any color. They also look great framed, mounted on a white or contrasting background.

3–32. Painted ¹⁄₃₂-inch-thick sheet aluminum was used to make this old German ornament.

**Old German Ornamental Silhouettes
Provided by Karl Gutbrod**

3–33. Pattern for Old German ornaments.

**Cut from ¹⁄₃₂" to ¹⁄₈" Thick Metal or Plywood.
Paint as Desired.**

Patterns Full Size or Change as Desired

3–34. Pattern for Old German ornaments.

Cut from ⅟₃₂" to ⅛" Thick Metal or Plywood.
Paint as Desired.

Pattern Full Size or Change as Desired

Old German Ornamental Silhouettes
Provided by Karl Gutbrod

CHAPTER 4

CROSSES

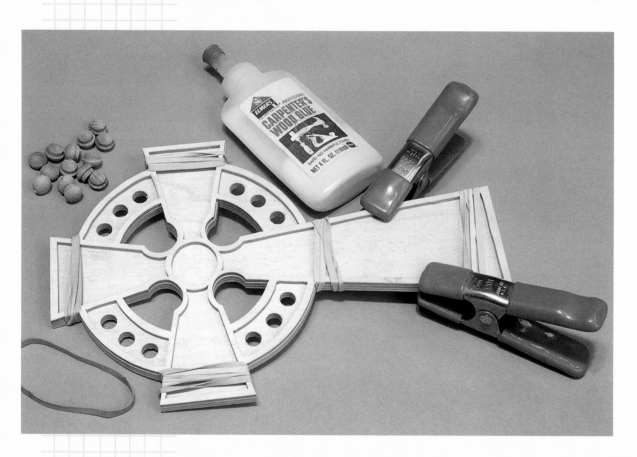

Among the patterns that highlight this chapter are those for key-chain crosses, simple and complex fretwork crosses, and crosses with interchangeable overlays, among which is a dimensional Celtic cross. Remember to consider the various design possibilities when patterns are enlarged or reduced and to always consider the potential for using materials other than wood.

Inexpensive metallic plastic figures of Jesus that are easily mounted to these projects are available from mail-order craft houses. If you intend to use cast figures, it is best to have them at hand before starting should it be necessary to size the pattern(s) accordingly.

Cross patterns can be created so they are simply flat with pierced inside openings, or made with overlays of contrasting wood or other material can be glued to their surfaces (4–1 and 4–2). Illus. 4–3 shows two patterns with flame designs that are specifically intended to be overlays. The eventual size of the design should determine the best thickness to use. Generally speaking, overlays of thinner stock look better than thick material. Illus. 4–4 and 4–5 show two wall plaques made from enlarged patterns.

KEY-CHAIN AND PENDANT CROSSES

4–1. Pendant cross of Texas ebony crafted by Dale Taylor. Secure a small screw eye ("up-eye") or pendant bail with instant or epoxy glue.

4–2. Patterns for key ring and pendant crosses.

Crosses
Designs for Key Rings or Pendants.
Enlarge Patterns for Sun Catchers.

4–3. Patterns for cross designs.

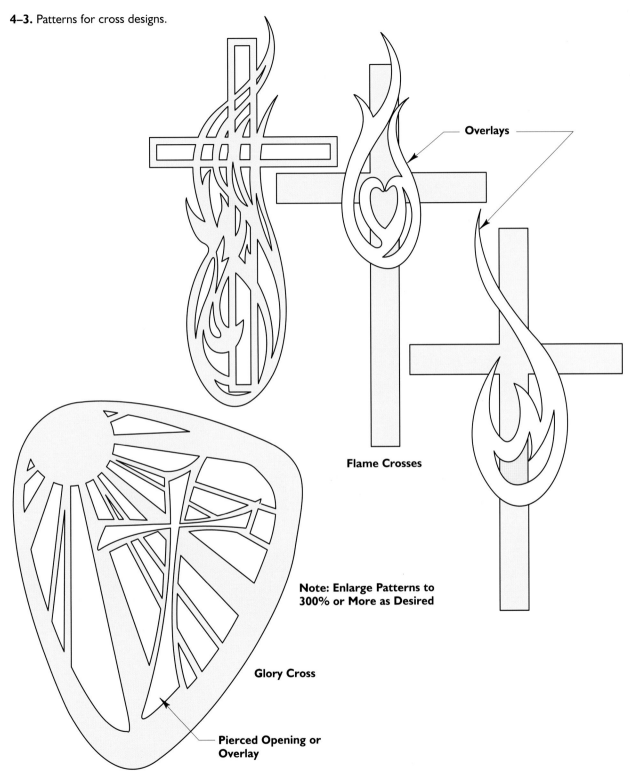

Overlays

Flame Crosses

Note: Enlarge Patterns to
300% or More as Desired

Glory Cross

Pierced Opening or
Overlay

Cross Designs by R. Stephan Toman

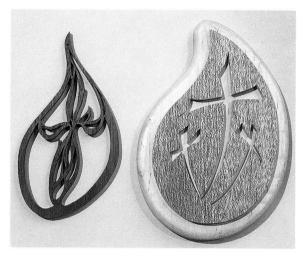

4–4. Left: Fretted flaming cross. Right: Enlarged ¼-inch-thick triple cross is a pierced overlay mounted to a ¾-inch-thick plaque with a routed edge.

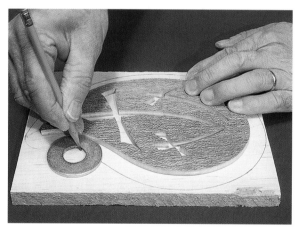

4–5. Drawing a line parallel to an irregular edge with the aid of a metal washer.

FRETWORK CROSSES

Use any material of choice in thicknesses from ⅛ to ¾ inch to make the crosses featured in **4–6** to **4–8**.

4–6. Beautiful fretwork cross made of ⅜-inch-thick walnut.

4–7. Pattern for fretwork cross.

**Cut from ⅛" to ½"
Thick Plywood**

4–8. Pattern for simple fretwork cross.

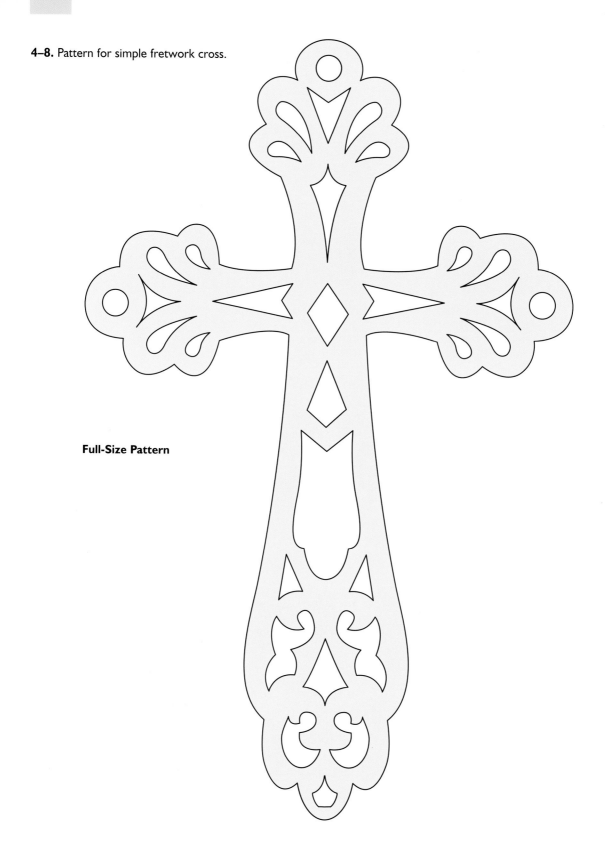

Full-Size Pattern

CROSSES WITH OVERLAYS AND CELTIC CROSS

Illus. **4–9** to **4–12** feature crosses that have the same overlay design. The Celtic cross shown in **4–13** (page 83) is much easier to make than it first appears, and therein lies the fun in making it. In fact, it is such an enjoyable project that I recommend making at least two or more crosses at the same time—one to keep and others to give.

MATERIAL REQUIRED PER CELTIC CROSS:

▦ *One piece of ¼ × 7 × 10½-inch plywood, for the backer.*

▦ *One piece of ⅛ × 7 × 10½-inch plywood, for border and overlay pieces.*

▦ *Twelve ⅜-inch-diameter screw-hole buttons*

▦ *Textured stone aerosol finish (your choice of color).*

4–9. Three crosses that can incorporate the same identical overlay or to which cast, metallic plastic figures can be mounted. Notice the two different sizes of plastic figures, both available by mail order or found in craft stores.

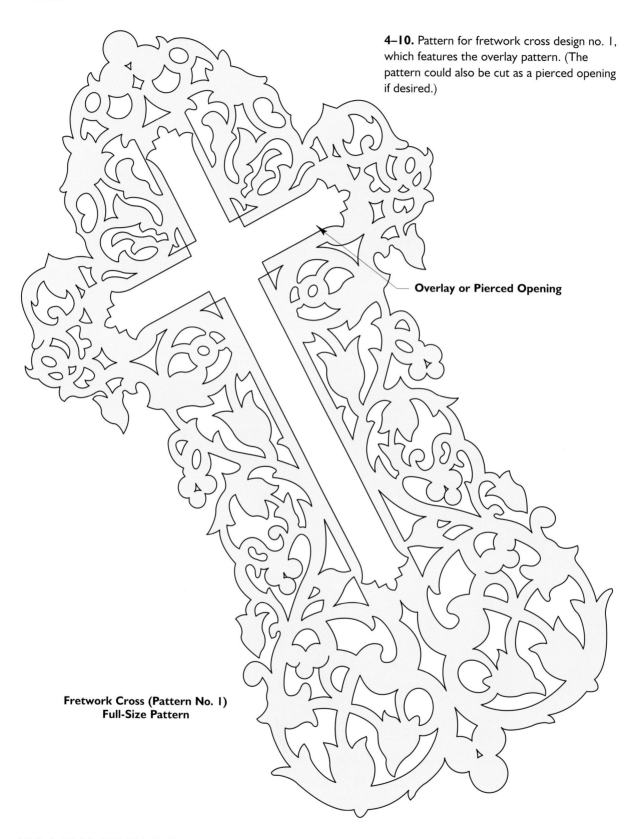

4–10. Pattern for fretwork cross design no. 1, which features the overlay pattern. (The pattern could also be cut as a pierced opening if desired.)

Overlay or Pierced Opening

**Fretwork Cross (Pattern No. 1)
Full-Size Pattern**

4–11. Pattern for cross design no. 2. Enlarge it 125 percent if using it with the overlay pattern from cross no. 1.

Enlarge Pattern 125%

Cross (Pattern No. 2)

4–12. Pattern for cross design no. 3. Enlarge it 125 percent if using it with the overlay pattern from cross no. 1.

Cross (Pattern No. 3)

Enlarge Pattern 125%

4–13. This Celtic cross involves some overlay work and a special spray-applied finish. The pattern is on page 85.

Construction Techniques for Celtic Cross:

1. Enlarge the pattern 125 percent, apply it to the top layer, and stack the overlay and backer pieces together.

2. With a ⅜-inch drill, drill 16 holes entirely through the stacked pad (12 holes for screw-hole buttons, and 4 holes in larger openings for blade-threading) (**4–14.**)

3. Saw out the four through inside openings.

4. Separate the backer and overlay pieces.

5. Set the backers aside and stack-saw the overlay pieces and border(s) (**4–15**).

6. Glue the outside border pieces to the backer(s) (**4–16**).

7. Glue in the screw-hole buttons (**4–17**).

8. Use a wood burner or a rotary tool to carve and reduce surfaces to simulate the interlacing of Celtic knot overlay pieces (**4–18** and **4–19**).

9. Glue all overlays in place.

10. Spray simulated stone effect (**4–20**) or apply the finish of your choice. Attach a sawtooth hanger to the rear.

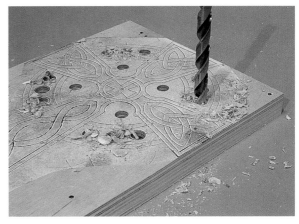

4–14. Drilling through a stack consisting of both a ⅛-inch-thick overlay and ¼-inch-thick backer material(s).

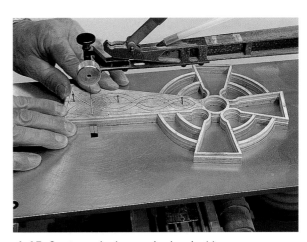

4–15. Sawing only the overlay border(s).

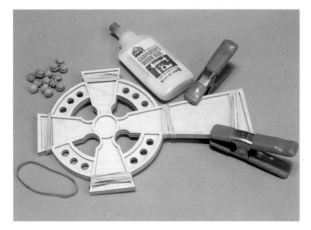

4–16. Gluing the border(s) to the backer(s).

4–17. Gluing in the screw-hole buttons.

4–18. Use a burning tool (or file) to make a separation line terminating the curved portions of the borders.

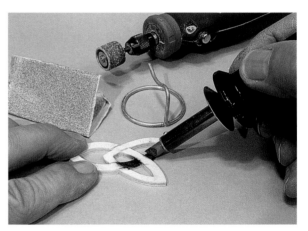

4–19. Tapering the thickness of one of the overlays to simulate the interlacing or the "over and under" effect of the Celtic knot.

4–20. Applying a textured stone finish with an aerosol spray.

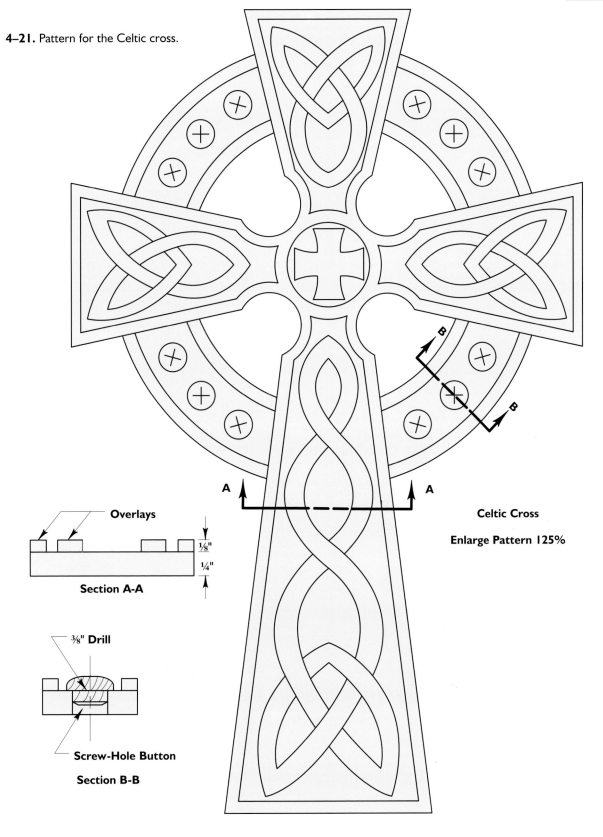

4–21. Pattern for the Celtic cross.

Overlays

⅛"
¼"

Section A-A

⅜" **Drill**

Screw-Hole Button

Section B-B

B

B

A   A

Celtic Cross

Enlarge Pattern 125%

CUTOUTS & SILHOUETTES

All of the projects in this chapter involve basic scroll-sawing skills. Six options to consider when making these projects are:

1. Enlarge or reduce patterns to satisfy personal preferences.

2. Use a variety of materials in suitable thicknesses.

3. Stack-saw a quantity of thin materials to make multiple pieces.

4. Finish as desired. Consider painting the stock before applying and cutting the pattern.

5. Mount the finished piece onto a contrasting plaque or panel backer or glue the backing material to the back of the project. Tagboard, felt, or "velvet board," mirrored acrylic plastic, and finished wood are a few possibilities.

6. Many of the designs are perfect for decorative overlays on boxes, furniture, and cabinetry.

The patterns and projects featured in this chapter do not have individual instructions.

5–1. Pierced silhouettes, left and lower.

5–2. Patterns for the pierced silhouettes.

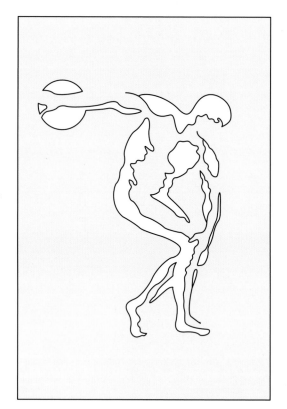

Pierced Silhouette

Pierced Silhouette

Enlarge Pattern to Suit

Design by Barbara McGivern

5–3. Pattern for bird and flower wreath.

Bird and Flower Wreath
Design by Barbara McGivern

Enlarge Pattern 154%

5–4. Patterns for cats and dog.

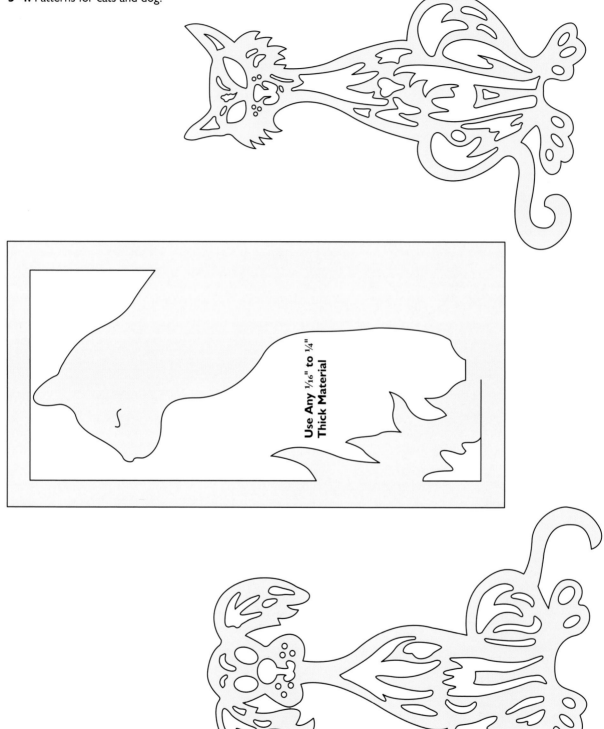

Use Any 1/16" to 1/4" Thick Material

5–5. Patterns for eagle and hummingbird.

Eagle
Design © 1999 by
H. Parsons

Hummingbird Design

5–6. Pattern for fretwork Viking.

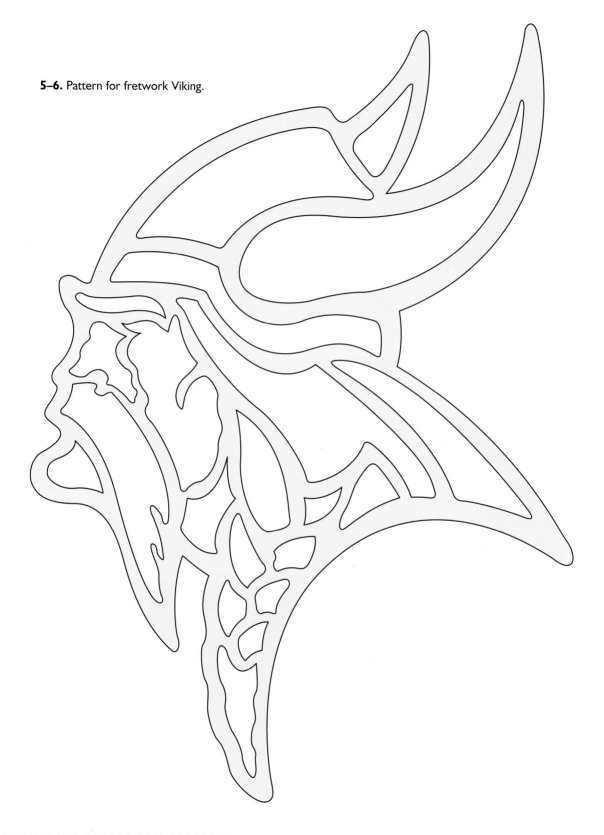

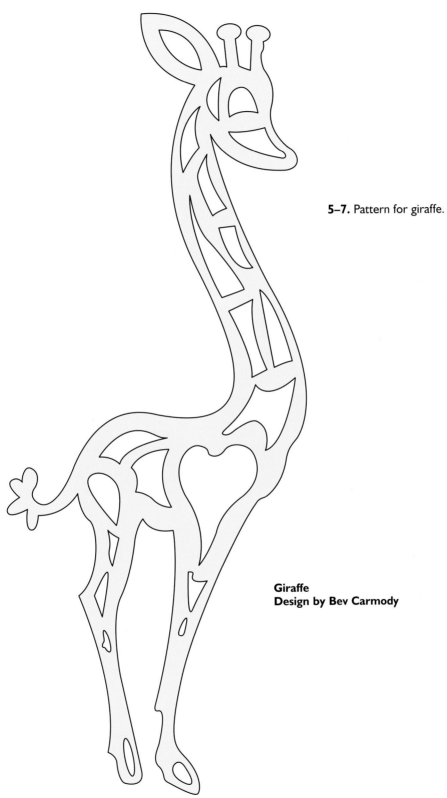

5–7. Pattern for giraffe.

Giraffe
Design by Bev Carmody

5–8. Pattern for thunderbird.

**Thunderbird
Design by Gail Hathaway**

5–9. Stylized horse cut from ⅛-inch unfinished plywood mounted to a stained plaque.

5–10. Fretwork cutouts.

5–11. Pattern for
stylized horse.

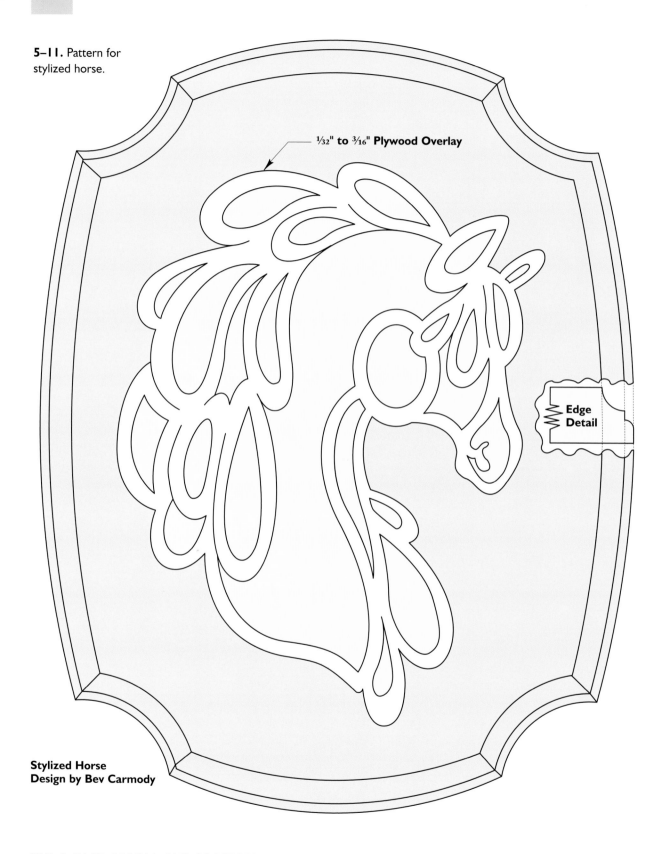

¹⁄₃₂" to ³⁄₁₆" Plywood Overlay

Edge
Detail

**Stylized Horse
Design by Bev Carmody**

5–12. Pattern for village door/window topper cutout.

Small Door/Window Topper
Design by Barb McGivern

Enlarge Pattern 200%

5–13. Pattern for phantom lady.

**Cut from ⅟₃₂" to ³⁄₁₆"
Thick Plywood**

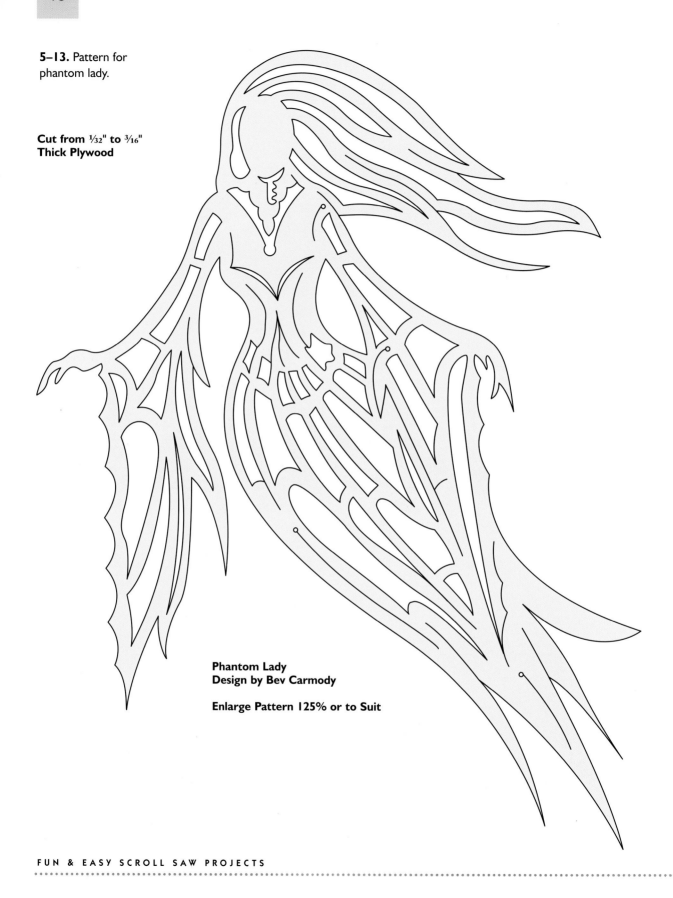

**Phantom Lady
Design by Bev Carmody**

Enlarge Pattern 125% or to Suit

5–14. Pattern for deer silhouette.

Silhouette
Design by Brian Dahlen
Use ⅛" to ¼" Thick Material

5–15. Deer scene and giant panda.

5–16. Pattern for giant panda.

Note: Cut from two pieces of ⅛" or ¼" plywood, one natural birch, one painted black. Cut inside openings of natural wood first and stack pieces to cut outside frame.

Design by Kyle Oram

Giant Panda
Enlarge Pattern 106%

5–17. Pattern for deer scene.

Enlarge Pattern 125%

Cut from ⅛" or ¼" Plywood

Optional Base, ¾" × 2" × 4"

**Deer Scene
Design by Gail Hathaway**

**Cedars on
Lake Michigan
Shoreline**

5–18. Patterns for shoreline and golfer.

5–19. Pattern for resting tiger.

Cut from ¹⁄₁₆" to ¼" Thick Plywood

Tiger

5–20. Pattern for lion.

Note: Cut from ¹⁄₁₆" to ¼" Thick Material

Optional: Glue Thin Contrasting Tagboard to Back

Enlarge Pattern 125% or More as Desired

Lion

5–21. Pattern for wolf scene.

Note: Cut from ¹⁄₁₆" to ¼" Thick Material   **Wolf**

Optional: Glue Thin Contrasting Tagboard to Back   **Enlarge Pattern 125% or More as Desired**

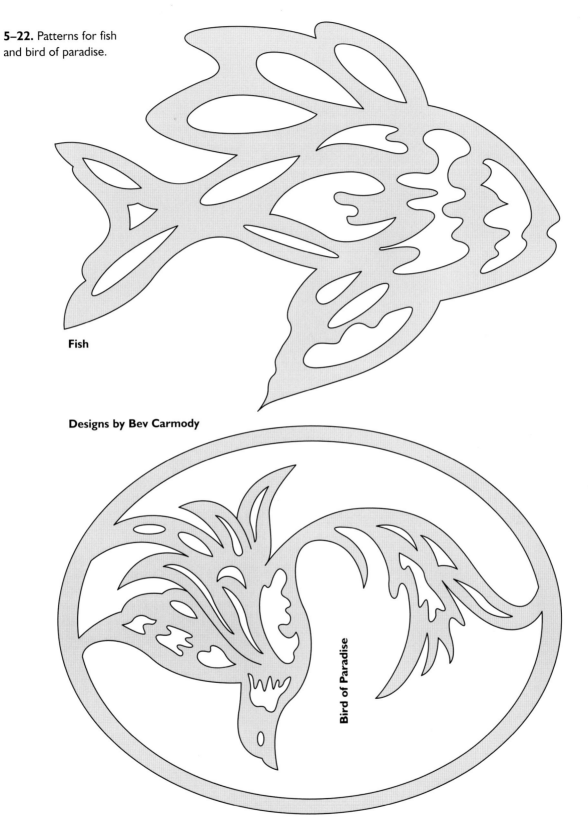

5–22. Patterns for fish and bird of paradise.

Fish

Designs by Bev Carmody

Bird of Paradise

5–23. Elvis and Marilyn sawn from ¹⁄₁₆-inch-thick birch plywood glued to stained or contrasting ¼-inch plywood backers that frame the overlays.

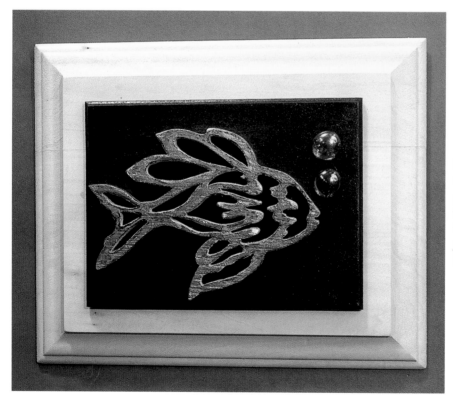

5–24. This fish cutout by Bev Carmody is painted with acrylic paints applied with a sponge, to simulate aged metal. Flat floral-accented marbles are glued to the backer to simulate bubbles.

5–25. Patterns for Elvis and Marilyn.

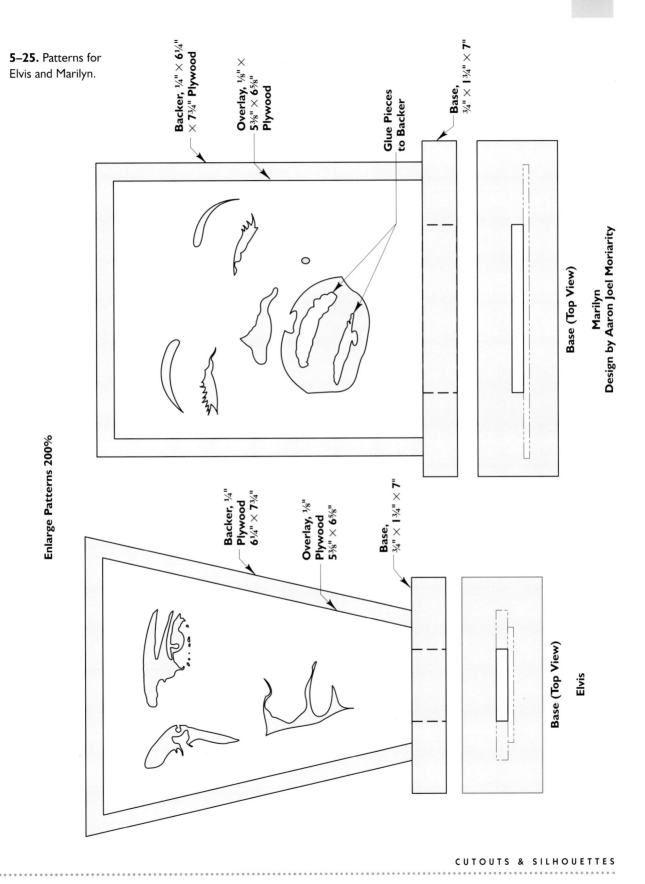

Enlarge Patterns 200%

Backer, $\frac{1}{4}$" × $6\frac{1}{4}$" × $7\frac{3}{4}$" **Plywood**

Overlay, $\frac{1}{8}$" × $5\frac{3}{8}$" × $6\frac{5}{8}$" **Plywood**

Glue Pieces to Backer

Base, $\frac{3}{4}$" × $1\frac{3}{4}$" × 7"

Base (Top View)

Marilyn
Design by Aaron Joel Moriarity

Backer, $\frac{1}{4}$" **Plywood** $6\frac{1}{4}$" × $7\frac{3}{4}$"

Overlay, $\frac{1}{8}$" **Plywood** $5\frac{3}{8}$" × $6\frac{5}{8}$"

Base, $\frac{3}{4}$" × $1\frac{3}{4}$" × 7"

Base (Top View)

Elvis

5–26. Horses sawn from ⅛-inch plywood, painted metallic gold, and glued to ⅛-inch black backer. Common washers were painted and glued to the corners for decorative accents. Designed and crafted by Bev Carmody.

5–27. One-eighth-inch acrylic mirror gives these and other simple scroll-sawn images an interesting and dramatic look.

5–28. Pattern for the fretwork horses.

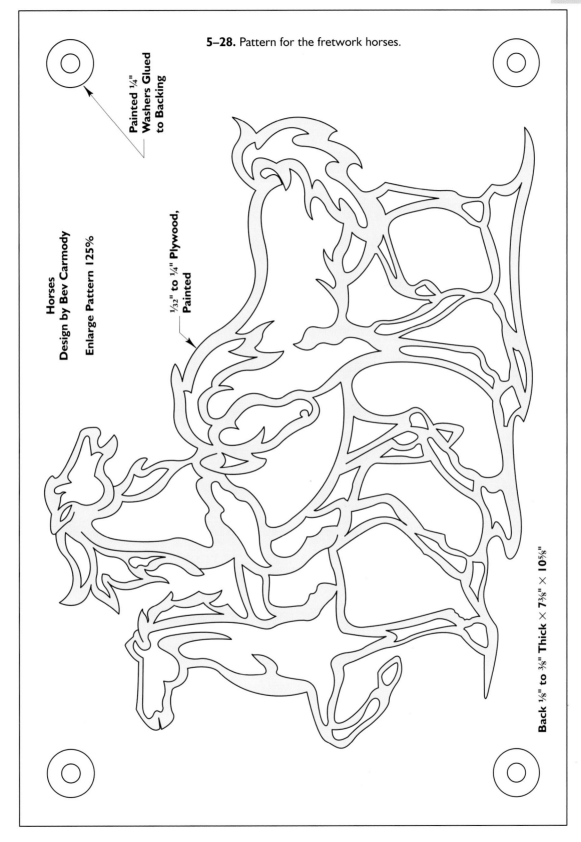

Painted ¼" Washers Glued to Backing

Horses
Design by Bev Carmody

Enlarge Pattern 125%

¹⁄₃₂" to ¼" Plywood, Painted

Back ⅛" to ⅜" Thick × 7⅜" × 10⅝"

5–29. Pattern for the horse sculpture.

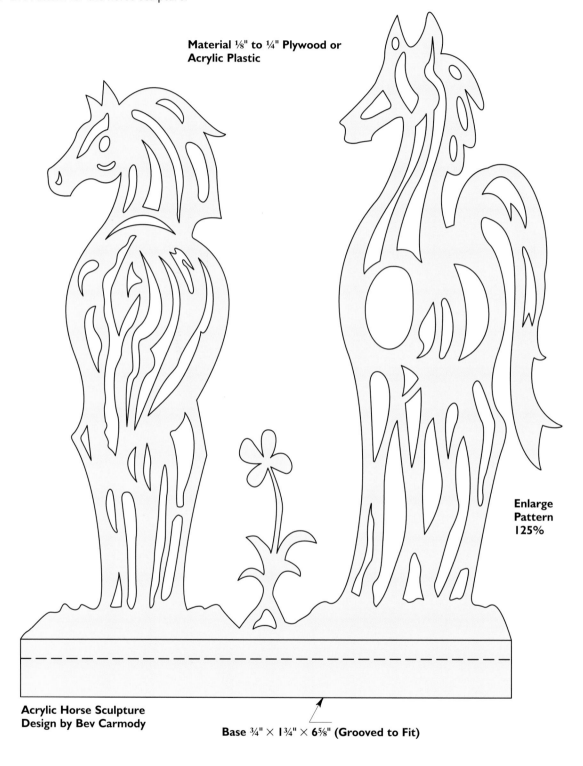

Material ⅛" to ¼" Plywood or Acrylic Plastic

Enlarge Pattern 125%

Acrylic Horse Sculpture Design by Bev Carmody

Base ¾" × 1¾" × 6⅝" (Grooved to Fit)

5–30. Patterns for cranes.

Enlarge Patterns 200%

Cranes
Designs by
Bev Carmody

5–31. Patterns for fantasy creatures.

**Cut from ⅛" to ¼"
Plywood or Acrylic
Plastic**

**Fantasy Designs
By Bev Carmody**

5–32. Pattern for three ladies.

**Enlarge Pattern
125%**

**Three Ladies
Design by Bev Carmody**

SHELVES

Classic ornate fretwork wall shelves have been popular scroll-sawing projects for decades. Three classic designs are included here along with a very simple flat surface shelf designed for receiving various overlays or heat-transferred artworks. All projects are best made with solid wood. Any suitable fine ¼-inch-thick hardwood can be used for the fretwork shelves. Light-colored, nonporous woods such as pine, maple, basswood, or birch accept heat-transferred designs very well. Basic scroll-sawing skills and general, fundamental woodworking techniques are all that are required.

FRETWORK SHELF (DESIGN NO. 1)

This fretwork shelf (**6–1** to **6–3**) requires three pieces of ¼-inch-thick hardwood: 8¾ × 10½ inches, 4¾ × 8½ inches, and 4⅜ × 4⅞ inches.

6–1. Fretwork shelf (design no. 1) made of ¼-inch-thick or finished mahogany.

6–2. Pattern for fretwork shelf (design no. 1) back piece.

Grain Direction

Fretwork Shelf (Design No. 1)

Enlarge Pattern 125%

6–3. Pattern for fretwork shelf (design no. 1) shelf and bracket.

Fretwork Shelf (Design No. 1)

Enlarge Pattern 125%

FRETWORK SHELF
(DESIGN NO. 2)

This shelf (**6–4** to **6–6**) requires three pieces of ¼-inch-thick hardwood: 6¾ × 9½ inches, 3½ × 6¾ inches, and 3¼ × 6½ inches.

6–4. Fretwork shelf (design no. 2) made of ¼- inch or finished mahogany.

6–5. Pattern for fretwork shelf (design no. 2) shelf.

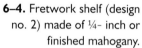

Grain Direction

Enlarge Pattern 125%

6–6. Patterns for fretwork shelf (design no. 2) back and bracket.

Fretwork Shelf (Design No. 2)

Use ¼" Solid Material

Enlarge Patterns 125%

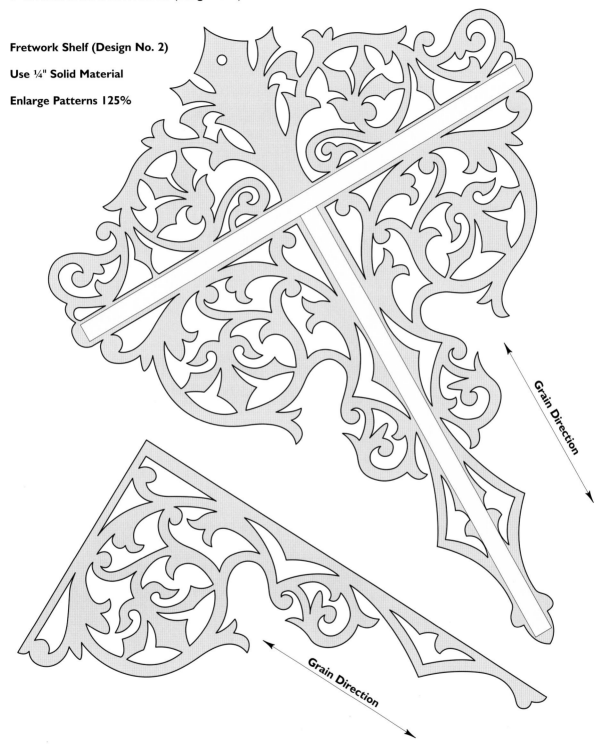

Grain Direction

Grain Direction

SIMPLE SOCCER SHELF

This easy-to-make shelf (**6–7** to **6–9**) requires one piece of wood ½ × 6 × 18 inches. It can be decorated in three different ways:

1. Left plain and finished without the soccer player art or other ornamentation.

2. Apply a contrasting glued-on wooden overlay of the soccer player or any suitable design of your choice.

3. Apply a heat transfer of any selected and appropriately sized art or graphic that has been copied on an office copy machine. The art is applied to the wood using the popular, new "transfer tool" techniques. Before photocopying the image of the soccer player, blacken it with a felt-tip marker. This will result in a darker transferred image. *Note:* The art for the sports clock project illustrated in Chapter 7 can also be modified and used for transfer-tool-applied decoration. Any printed image that can be copied on a photocopy machine can be transferred to wood.

Using the transfer tool is easy. Make a photocopy of the image with a photocopy machine and size it to suit. Place the photocopied image face down and apply heat with the transfer tool as shown in **6–8**. Notice that the final image will be a reversed transfer of the original.

6–7. This easy-to-make shelf can be decorated with any suitable thin plywood overlay or, more quickly, decorated with an electrically heated "image transfer tool" that transfers photocopied graphics to wood surfaces.

6–8. The transfer tool in use.

6–9. Plan and pattern for the simple soccer shelf.

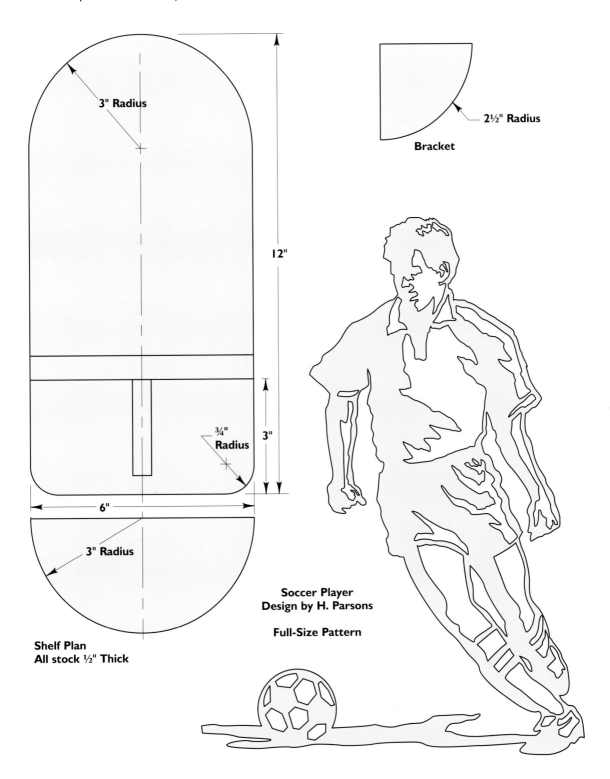

3" Radius

2½" Radius

Bracket

12"

¾"
Radius

3"

6"

3" Radius

Shelf Plan
All stock ½" Thick

Soccer Player
Design by H. Parsons

Full-Size Pattern

CHAPTER 7
CLOCKS

Scroll-sawn clocks that accept commercially available, battery-driven fit-ups or inserts are fascinating and easy projects to make. This chapter provides eight entirely different designs that incorporate basic woodworking techniques with a variety of wood materials.

CHEVY CLOCK

This project (**7–1** and **7–3**) requires one piece of ⅛- or ¼-inch-thick plywood that is 5⅞ × 7½ inches and a ¾ × 1½ × 5¾-inch base piece grooved ⅜ inch deep to receive the plywood. Purchase a mini-clock insert and paint or finish the project as desired.

7–1. Ye Old Chevy Clock made of painted ⅛-inch plywood with a mahogany base.

MINI FRETWORK CLOCK

This clock (**7–2** and **7–4**) is made of any suitable solid ¼-inch-thick wood. The pattern, however, is easily modified for use with ³⁄₁₆- or ⅛-inch-thick wood as well. Only three pieces are required: two 2 ⅛ × 2½-inch base pieces and one 2⅜ × 7¾-inch piece.

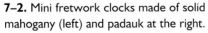

7–2. Mini fretwork clocks made of solid mahogany (left) and padauk at the right.

7–3. Pattern for Ye Old Chevy Clock.

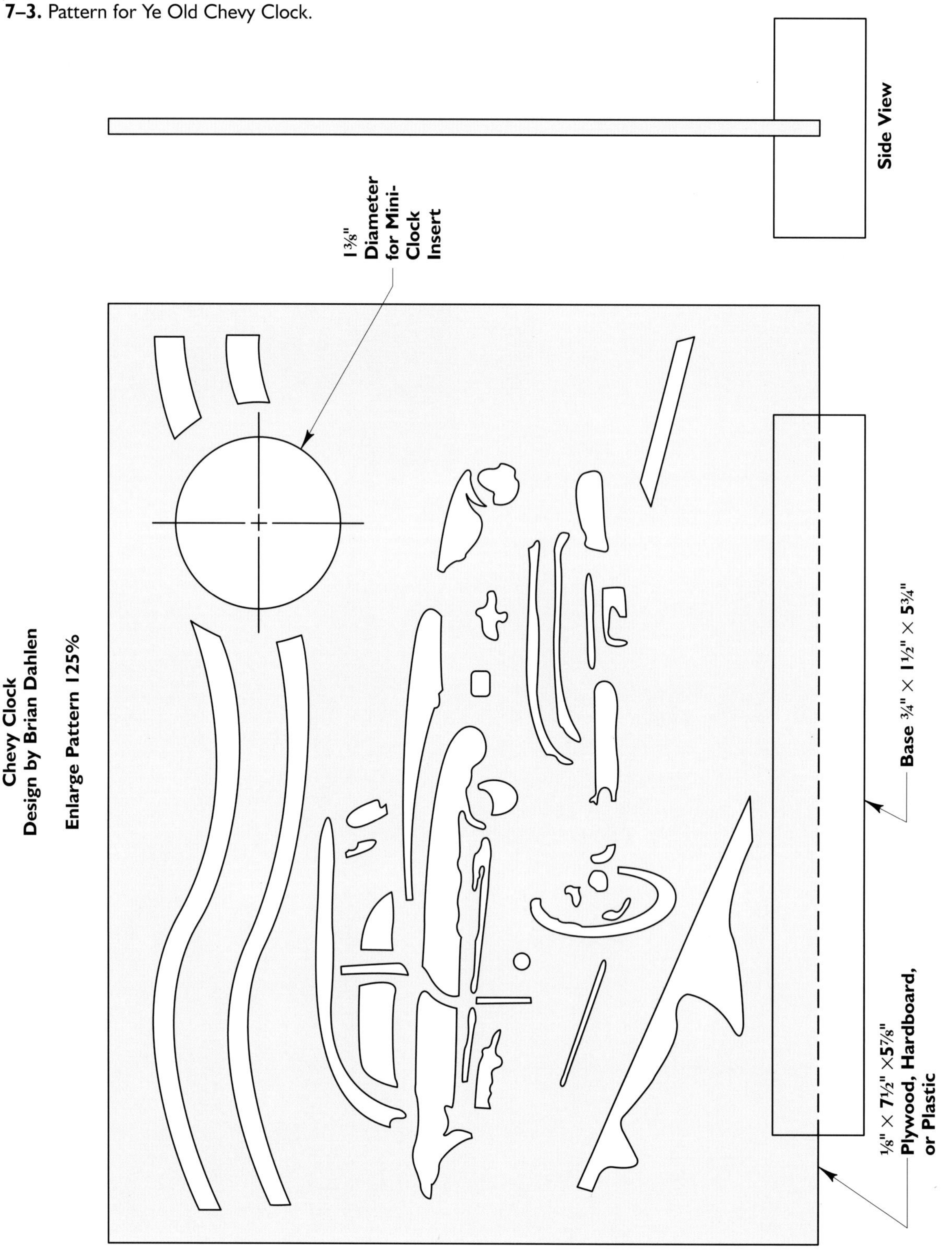

Side View

1³⁄₈" **Diameter for Mini-Clock Insert**

Chevy Clock Design by Brian Dahlen

Enlarge Pattern 125%

Base ³⁄₄" × 1¹⁄₂" × 5³⁄₄"

¹⁄₈" × 7¹⁄₂" ×5⁵⁄₈" **Plywood, Hardboard, or Plastic**

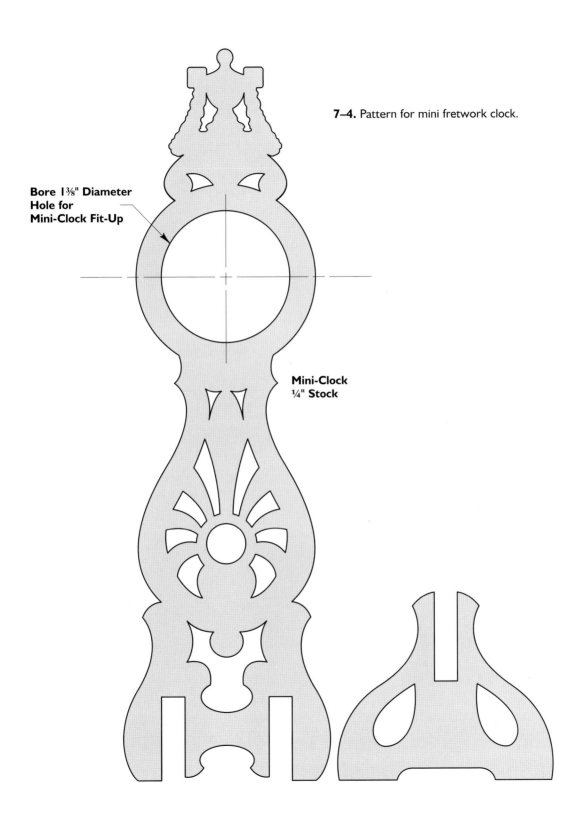

7–4. Pattern for mini fretwork clock.

Bore 1⅜" Diameter Hole for Mini-Clock Fit-Up

Mini-Clock ¼" Stock

DRAGON CLOCK

This clock (**7–5** and **7–7**) is made from one piece of ¼ × 7½ × 8¾-inch plywood and two base pieces of ¾ × 2¼ × 3¼-inch softwood. Paint the dragon green, the base piece gray to simulate rock, and the fire-breath piece a bright red or fluorescent orange. This project is designed for a 2-inch-diameter clock insert.

7–5. Dragon clock made from painted Baltic-birch plywood sandwiched between two ¾-inch-thick pine base pieces.

CORMORANTS

This simple black-and-white project (**7–6** and **7–8**) requires the following materials:

One ¾ × 8 × 13¼-inch piece, for the backer

One ⅜ × 3 × 7-inch piece, for the rocks

One ½ × 2½ × 7-inch piece, for the rocks

One ¼ × 2⅜ × 6-inch piece, for the birds

Two ⅛ × 1¾ × 9-inch pieces, for the frame

Two ⅛ × 1¾ × 14-inch pieces, for the frame

One clock insert 3⅜ inches in diameter

7–6. Cormorants clock.

7–7. Pattern for dragon clock.

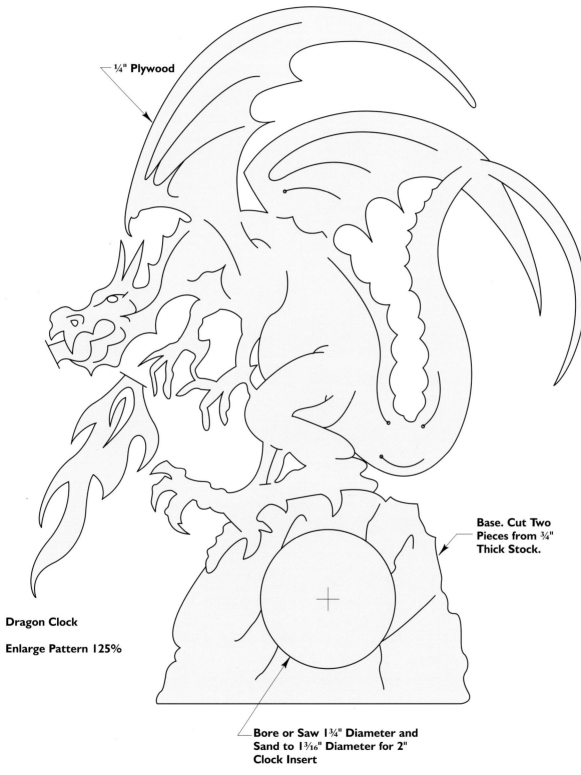

¼" Plywood

Base. Cut Two
Pieces from ¾"
Thick Stock.

Dragon Clock

Enlarge Pattern 125%

Bore or Saw 1¾" Diameter and
Sand to 1³⁄₁₆" Diameter for 2"
Clock Insert

7–8. Pattern for the cormorants clock.

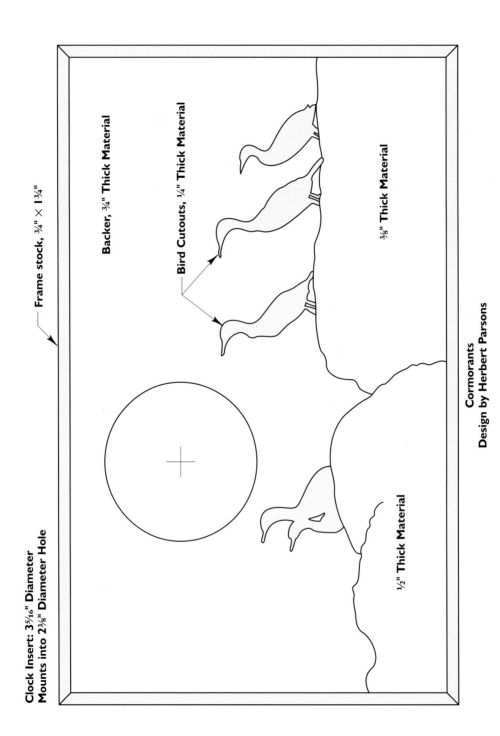

Clock Insert: 3⁵/₁₆" Diameter
Mounts into 2³/₈" Diameter Hole

Frame stock, ³/₄" × 1³/₄"

Backer, ³/₄" Thick Material

Bird Cutouts, ¼" Thick Material

³/₈" **Thick Material**

½" **Thick Material**

Cormorants
Design by Herbert Parsons

Enlarge Pattern 200%

OVAL CLOCK

This clock (**7–9** and **7–12**) is designed for the new oval-shaped clock inserts that have recently become available. This project, if made without feet, becomes a wall clock. The standing clock requires one piece of ½ × 6½ × 7½-inch solid wood and two ¾ × ¾ × 2-inch foot pieces. Use ⅝- or ¾-inch-thick stock for a wall-hung clock. The clock insert extends ⅝ inch behind the rim or face of the clock.

7–9. Oval clock in oil-finished natural oak.

SLAB CLOCK

The slab clock (**7–10**, **7–11**, and **7–13**) features wide, pierced-line work cut with the largest spiral blades available. Although one manufacturer labels its largest blade a no. 6 and another manufacturer calls its a no. 8, all cut close to the same width kerf, almost .050 inch. All that is required is a diagonally cut slab, sometimes called a "log slice," that is available from a craft store, or use any board of suitable size. *Tip:* First select the stock and then size the pattern to the slab or board and order a clock insert of proportional size. Don't "fret" if you do not follow the pattern lines precisely. This project actually looks best if cut with a crude-looking, primitive style (**7–11**).

7–10. The slab clock features pierced line work in this basswood slab available from craft stores.

7–11. Close-up view that shows the wide kerf and rough-sawn surface produced with large spiral scroll-saw blades.

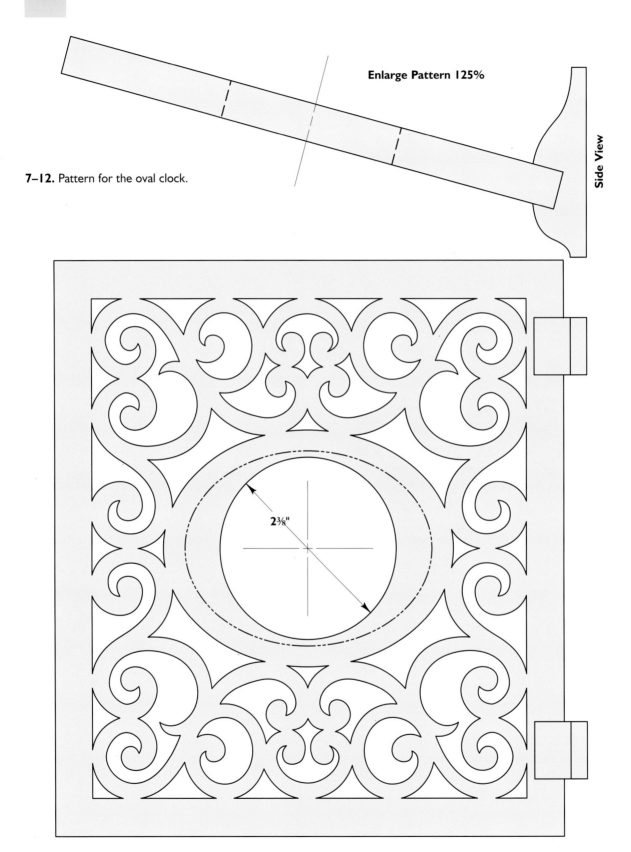

Enlarge Pattern 125%

Side View

7–12. Pattern for the oval clock.

2⅜"

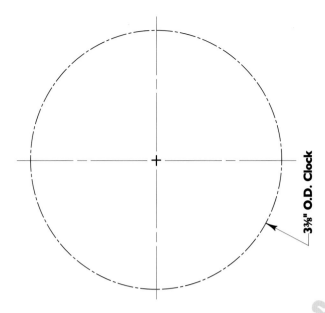

3⅜" O.D. Clock

7–13. Pattern for slab clock line art.

Enlarge Pattern 125% or to Suit

Designed by Gail Hathaway

SPORTS CLOCK

The sports clock (**7–14** to **7–17**) is of super-simple two-piece construction with a choice of five moderately challenging track and tennis figures. The clock face is made from a piece of ⅛ × 9-inch-square birch plywood. Bore the hour and clock shaft holes through the face only. Drill the clock shaft hole through both pieces. The design is intended to be pierce-cut through the face so the holes and design expose the dark backer. Use a 2/0 blade. Other design options, however, can be conceived by the scroll-sawer. The backer is made from one piece of ¼ × 9¾ × 9¾-inch dark or stained plywood.

An alternate clock face can be created with the use of the transfer-tool technique shown and described with the shelf project on page 122. The soccer player design is not "pierceable," but could be either cut out from ¹⁄₁₆- or ⅛-inch plywood and used as an overlay on the clock face, or a darkened photocopy of it could be simply applied to the surface with the transfer tool.

Select a clock movement with a 4¼-inch minute hand length.

7–14. The sports clock consists of pierced ⅛-inch-thick birch plywood over a ¼-inch stained plywood backer.

7–15. A close-up look at typical sawing detail. This design features a likeness of famous runner Steve Prefontaine in reverse or pierced-cut silhouette.

7–16. Patterns for the sports clock.

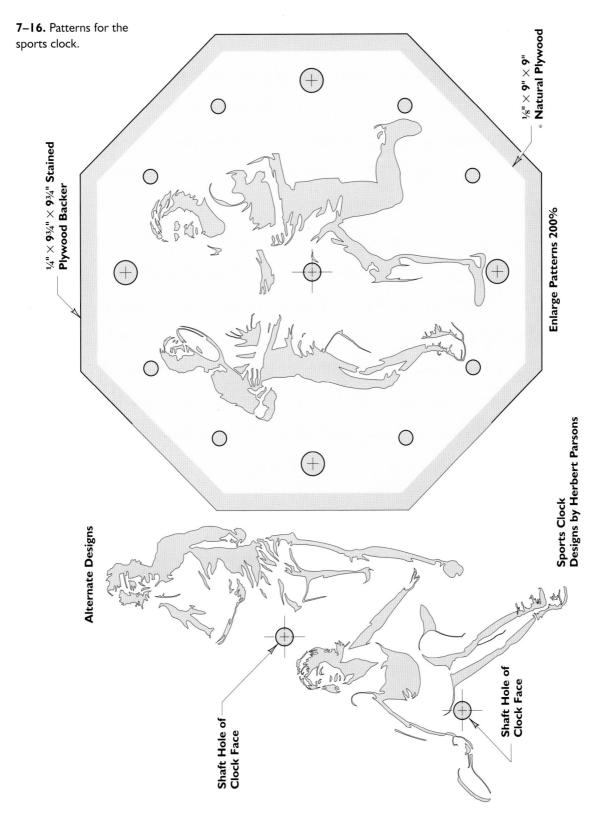

¼" × 9¾" × 9¾" **Stained Plywood Backer**

⅛" × 9" × 9" **Natural Plywood**

Enlarge Patterns 200%

Sports Clock
Designs by Herbert Parsons

Alternate Designs

Shaft Hole of Clock Face

Shaft Hole of Clock Face

7–17. Pattern for the sports clock.

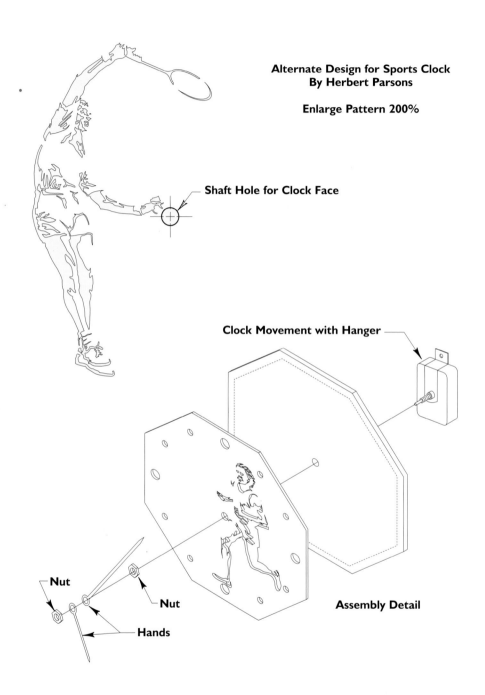

**Alternate Design for Sports Clock
By Herbert Parsons**

Enlarge Pattern 200%

Shaft Hole for Clock Face

Clock Movement with Hanger

Nut

Nut

Hands

Assembly Detail

TIME AND TEMPERATURE PLAQUE

One piece of fine ¾ × 9½ × 14½-inch hardwood is required to make this project (**7–18** and **7–19**). The construction procedures are fairly routine, except for making the ⅛-inch-wide × ⅜-inch-deep rabbet in the back for the 1½ × 5-inch carded thermometer purchased from a craft supply house. This project calls for the use of a router to make the rabbet and edge round-over cuts. Since most standard rabbeting router bits cut ⅜ inch wide, make the ⅛-inch rabbet using either of the two methods described as follows:

1. Scroll-saw all inside openings including the thermometer opening area following the lines exactly as given on the pattern (**7–19**). Next, cut small strips of ¼ × ¾-inch wood and temporarily line the inside of the opening with them as shown in **7–20**, to reduce the size of the opening. Use double-faced tape to hold the strips in place. Now, rout all around the back with a ⅜-inch rabbeting bit as usual. Remove the strips and a perfect, ⅛-inch-wide rabbet is the result, but you will still need to chisel the inside corners square.

2. This is a safer technique. Before applying the pattern, draw the thermometer opening lines ¼ inch smaller all around the inside of the existing pattern lines. Cut out the smaller-sized opening with a scroll saw. Now, using a ⅜-inch rabbeting bit, rout the rabbet around the back side. Flip the workpiece over and use a scroll saw to cut the thermometer opening a second time, but this time cutting on the lines originally given on the pattern.

Round over all edges (**7–21** to **7–23**); however, do not round over the inside of the hole for the clock insert. Sand all surfaces (**7–24**) and finish as desired. Install the thermometer.

7–18. This time and temperature plaque made of ¾-inch walnut requires cutting an unusual ⅛-inch-wide rabbet around the opening to receive the thermometer card.

7–19. Pattern for the time and temperature plaque.

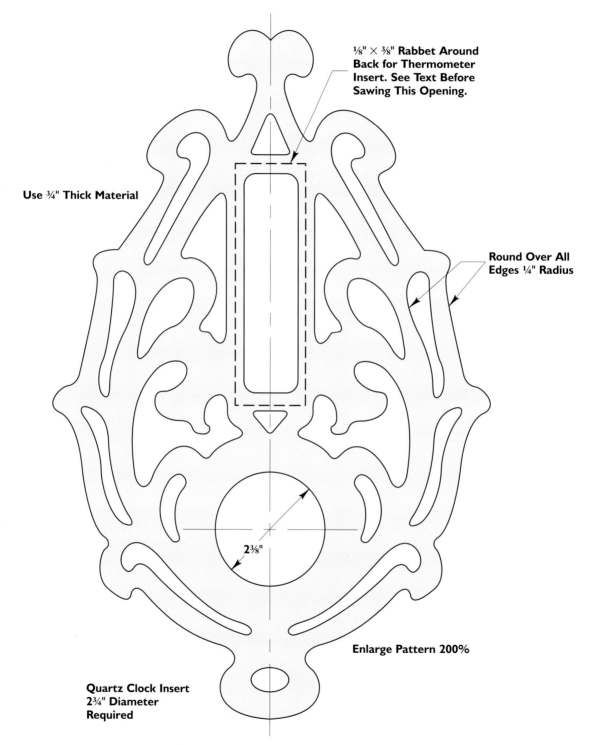

⅛" × ⅜" **Rabbet Around Back for Thermometer Insert. See Text Before Sawing This Opening.**

Use ¾" Thick Material

Round Over All Edges ¼" Radius

2⅜"

Enlarge Pattern 200%

Quartz Clock Insert 2¾" Diameter Required

Time and Temperature Wall Plaque

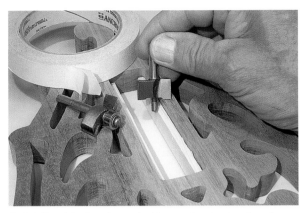

7–20. Double-faced tape holds small strips in place for routing to create a ⅛-inch rabbet when using a typical ⅜-inch rabbeting bit.

7–21. Use a round-over bit with a integral pilot as shown to round over the clock's edges.

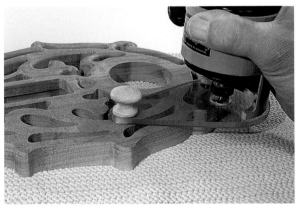

7–22. Rounding over edges with a router.

7–23. A close-up of the edge. A sharp bit, multiple passes, and a soft horizontal feed should produce clean cuts with few if any burns.

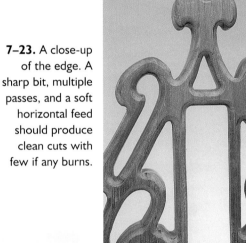

7–24. Sanding is easy with the flutter wheel. Notice how tape holds the trigger switch of this variable speed drill; the switch is turned on at the best speed choice.

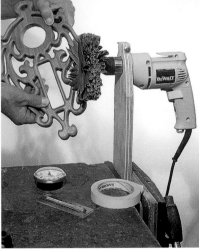

CANDLESTICKS

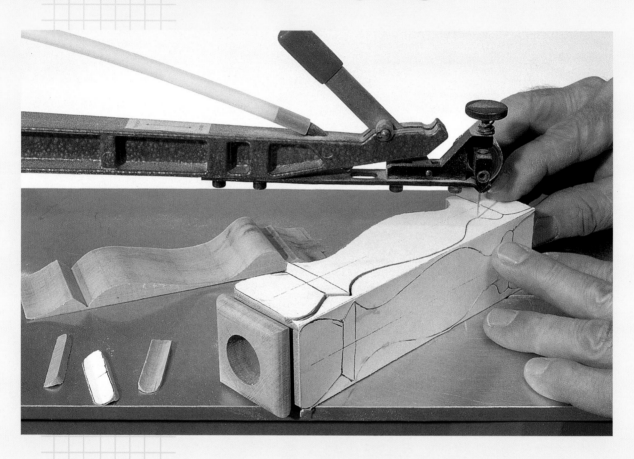

At first glance, these full-size candlesticks (**8–1** and **8–3**) do not look as if they were made with a scroll saw. Both designs are made in exactly the same way, that is, employing compound-sawing techniques, also called three-dimensional sawing or double-sawing by some experts. Essentially, the process involves a double pattern (**8–2** and **8–4**) that is used to saw designs from two adjoining surfaces. The basic technique is briefly described and illustrated here. If more information is necessary, refer to the *New Scroll Saw Handbook* for a complete discussion of the process.

To make the compound candlesticks requires a scroll saw with a minimum 1⅞-inch-thickness-cutting capacity. Recommended blades are the new "thick wood" type which do in fact cut thick wood very nicely. Otherwise, use a large skip-tooth blade in the no. 9 to no. 12 range.

CANDLESTICKS
(DESIGN NO. 1)

Each candlestick (**8–1** and **8–2**) consists of three individual pieces: one piece 1¾ inch square × 5½-inch stem, and a two-piece base consisting of one piece ¼ × 2¼ inches square on top of a piece ½ × 3¼ inches square.

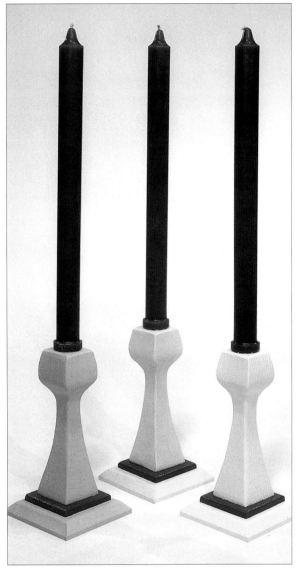

8–1. Candlestick design no. 1 consists of a square compound-sawn stem attached to a built-up, two-piece base.

8–2. Pattern for candlestick (design no. 1).

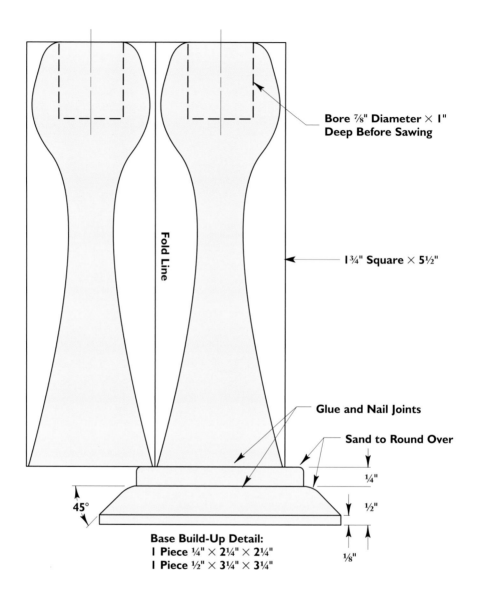

Bore ⅞" Diameter × 1" Deep Before Sawing

Fold Line

1¾" Square × 5½"

Glue and Nail Joints

Sand to Round Over

45°

¼"

½"

⅛"

Base Build-Up Detail:
1 Piece ¼" × 2¼" × 2¼"
1 Piece ½" × 3¼" × 3¼"

Candlestick (Design No. 1)
Base Build-up Detail

Enlarge Patterns 125%

CANDLESTICKS (DESIGN NO. 2)

This design (**8–3** and **8–4**) is made with two different stem lengths: 1¾ inch square × 7¾ inches long and 1¾ inch square × 5¾ inches long. The bases consist of one piece ¼ inch thick × 2¼ inches square on top of a piece ¾ inch thick × 3¾ inches square.

8–3. Candlestick design no. 2 is a little more challenging. This candlestick is made in two sizes, and painted in wild colors of choice. It also has square compound-sawn tenons that fit mortise openings cut into the two-piece bases.

8–4. Patterns for candlestick (design no. 2).

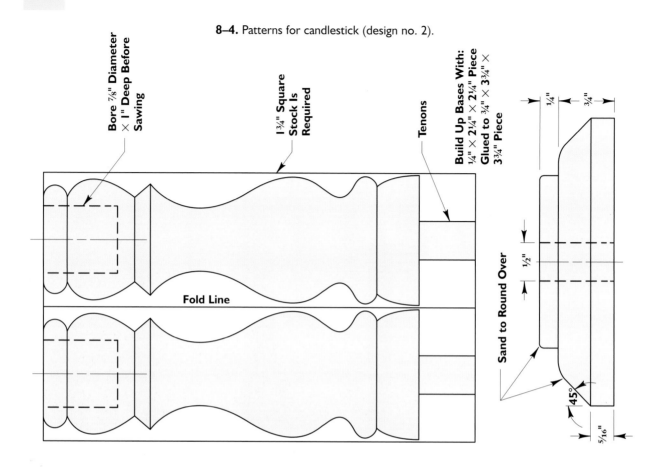

Bore ⅞" Diameter × 1" Deep Before Sawing

1¾" Square Stock Is Required

Tenons

Build Up Bases With:
¼" × 2¼" × 2¼" Piece
Glued to ¾" × 3¾" × 3¾" Piece

Fold Line

Sand to Round Over

¼"

¾"

½"

45°

5/16"

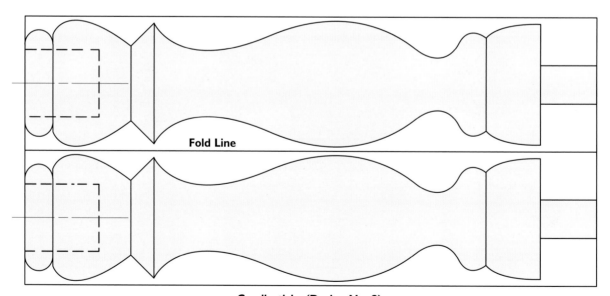

Fold Line

Candlesticks (Design No. 2)

Enlarge Patterns 125%

GENERAL CONSTRUCTION TIPS:

1. Square the table to the blade and ensure that the blade is well-tensioned.

2. Scissor-cut around the outside of the pattern's straight lines, leaving them joined at the "fold lines."

3. Carefully apply the pattern(s), positioning them so there is equal waste at the edges.

4. Use a drill press and vise to end-bore the ⅞-inch-diameter holes 1 inch deep.

5. Saw the first side profile, making two continuous cuts from top to bottom, so the waste pieces remain as a single "slab" (**8–5** and **8–6**).

6. Strategically place small drops of glue on the waste pieces (or wrap them with masking tape) and reposition the waste pieces against the workpiece (**8–6**).

7. Rotate the workpiece 90 degrees and follow the cutting lines of the second pattern, which now faces up (**8–7**).

8. Make the bottom pieces and attach the stem pieces.

9. Paint or finish the project as desired. Acrylic paints were applied to the candlesticks shown here.

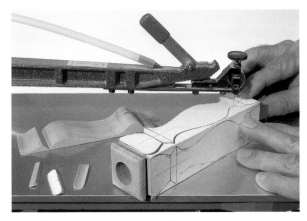

8–5. Cutting the pattern(s) applied to two adjoining surfaces with continuous lengthwise cuts.

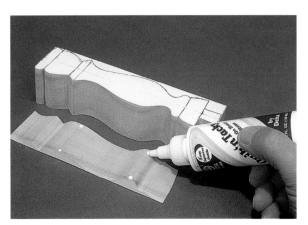

8–6. Use spots of glue (or a wrap of masking tape) to reattach the waste cutouts before making the second series of cuts with the workpiece rotated 90 degrees.

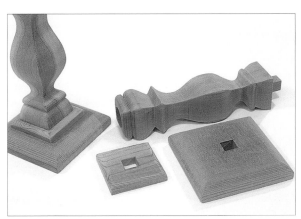

8–7. The parts ready to paint and assemble.

BOXES

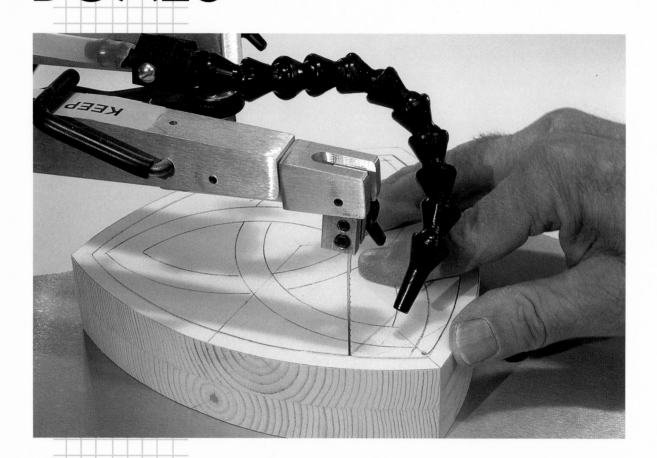

Basic scroll-sawing techniques are employed to create and decorate various kinds and shapes of easy-to-make boxes. This chapter first shows how to make a secret hiding compartment inside an old book. Next, I show how to make and decorate a tissue box with overlays. The overall techniques can be utilized also to make other boxes or projects. Finally, you will learn a simple and foolproof way to make boxes with heart, triangular, and other shapes by gluing a very thin plywood bottom (that is hardly visible) to scroll-sawn side walls of the shape you wish to create.

SECRET STORAGE BOOK

The scroll saw is perfect for making this unusual project (**9–1** to **9–4**). All that is needed is an old, unwanted book of any suitable size and some scrap plywood. First, prepare the book: Turn the covers back to back and restrain them with a rubber band. Next, sandwich the pages to be cut between two pieces of scrap plywood (**9–2**). Use any fairly coarse scroll-saw blade. *Tip:* Drive nails through the "sand-wich" while it is held over a flat steel surface. This peens the nail points holding the sandwich tight, and the nail points will not scratch the scroll-saw table. Freehand-cut an irregular-shaped cutting line (**9–3**). You can make a straight-line, rectangular cut, but keep in mind that the results will not look good if the opening's edges are not sawn exactly parallel to the lines of page type or the edge margins (**9–4**).

9–1. A secret compartment in an old book is cut out with the scroll saw.

9–2. With both covers turned back, nail the inside pages together sandwiched between two pieces of waste plywood. Notice the metal plate.

9–3. Sawing the free-form opening through the prepared "sandwich."

9–4. The completed compartment, neatly cut, and the stack of waste.

OVERLAID TISSUE BOX

To make this tissue box (**9–5** to **9–8**), begin with construction of the simple pine or basswood box made from ¼-inch-thick solid wood: Four ¼ × 5 × 5¾-inch sides and one 5-inch square top piece are required. *Note*: These tissue boxes can be purchased premade from craft and hobby stores. Use ⅟32- or ⅟16-inch-thick Baltic-birch plywood for the overlays. It should be 5 inches wide × either 4½ or 5½ inches long, depending upon the overlay design choice. Stack-saw the four overlays. Next, glue them to the sides of the assembled box. Using spray adhesive is the easiest method (**9–8**). Soften the sharp edges with a flutter wheel (**9–9**). *Important*: Use a clear, nongloss finish that is compatible with the adhesive. The solvents in some finishes, such as Danish oil, will dissolve certain spray adhesives.

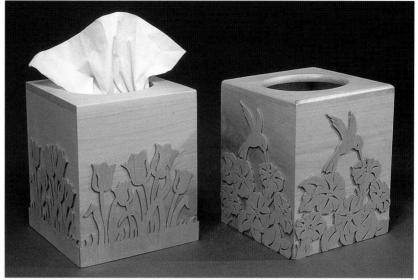

9–5. Thin Baltic-birch plywood overlays provide a subtle contrast and nice relief on these basswood tissue boxes.

Sides: ¼" × 5" × 5¾"

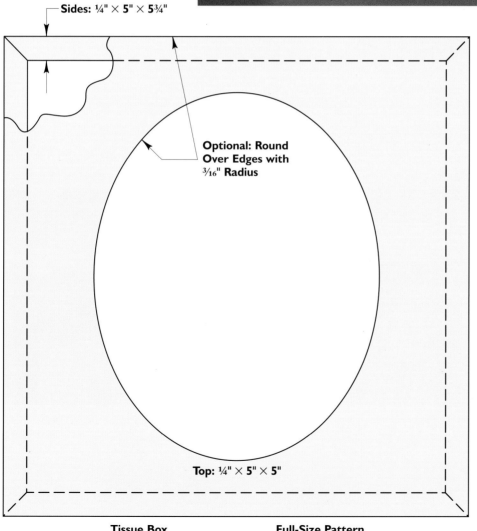

Optional: Round Over Edges with ³⁄₁₆" Radius

9–6. Pattern for the basic tissue box.

Top: ¼" × 5" × 5"

Tissue Box   **Full-Size Pattern**

9–7. Pattern for overlay no. 1 (tulips).

Tissue Box Overlay Full-Size Pattern

9–8. Spray the adhesive directly at a right angle to the surface to minimize glue build-up at the edges.

9–9. Using the flutter wheel to soften sharp edges.

9–10. Pattern for overlay no. 2 (hummingbird).

Tissue Box Overlay Full-Size Pattern.

HEART BOX

This project (**9–11** to **9–13**) involves basic scroll-sawing skills. Four pieces of material are required: one thick-wood piece for the box sides (walls) in a size that is just under the maximum sawing-thickness capacity of your scroll saw and 7½ inches square; a one-piece ¼-inch-thick, 7½-inch-square cover; a lid backer of ⅛-inch-thick, 7-inch-square plywood; and one bottom piece of ¹⁄₁₆- or ⅛-inch-thick, 7½-inch-square plywood. The general procedures are:

1. Make two photocopies of the pattern: one for sawing the lid and one for cutting the walls from the thick wood (**9–12**).

2. Cut the parts as specified on the pattern (**9–13**).

3. Sand and then glue the thin plywood bottom to the box wall all around it. Bevel back the edge as shown in **9–13**.

4. Finish the fretted lid pieces separately and paint the backer. Finish all surfaces of all pieces.

5. Tack the lid back to the fretted lid. Do not glue it. Gluing might induce warpage with changes of environmental humidity.

9–11. This heart box is a good example of a simple technique employing the scroll saw to cut irregular shapes to create boxes.

9–12. Making true vertical and parallel line cuts in thick wood requires a quality scroll saw, a good blade, and sufficient tension.

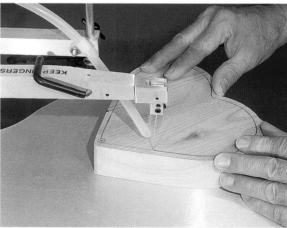

Fretted Heart Box

Enlarge Pattern 125%

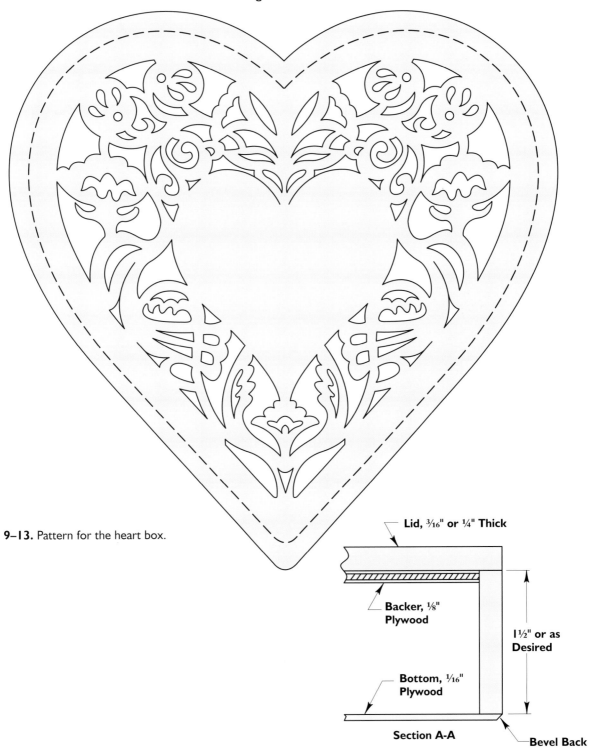

9–13. Pattern for the heart box.

Lid, 3/16" or 1/4" Thick

Backer, 1/8" Plywood

1½" or as Desired

Bottom, 1/16" Plywood

Section A-A

Bevel Back

CELTIC BOX

The Celtic knot relief carved on the lid of this box (**9–14** and **9–15**) is not as difficult as it looks. It is not a separate sculptured overlay, but a shaped, raised relief created by bevel-sawing and simple rounding-over carving technique. To make the box as shown requires four pieces of ¾ × 7¼-inch-square plywood, and one piece of ¹⁄₁₆- or ⅛-inch-thick plywood for a bottom piece. Another piece of ⅛-inch-thick, 7-inch square plywood is required for under the lid to keep it in place. Refer to the *New Scroll Saw Handbook* for an in-depth discussion of the bevel-sawing technique used to make the lid of this box.

GENERAL CONSTRUCTION TIPS:

1. Make two copies of the pattern: one to saw the box walls and another to bevel-cut the sawn lid pieces.

2. If the scroll saw has sufficient thickness-cutting capacity, glue the three pieces for the box walls together. If not, glue two layers together and add the third piece, sawn separately, later.

3. Cut the outside triangular perimeter of the lid piece with the table set square to the blade.

4. Make a small circular test cut in scrap with the saw table tilted 2½ to 3½ degrees with a no. 4 or 5 blade. Make trial-and-error table-tilt settings until the circular scrap cutout becomes wedged against the kerf walls at about a ⅜-inch relief to the background when pushed either up or down. Make more practice bevel-sawn cutouts until you know which feeding direction will produce either a relief or recessed surface (**9–16**).

5. Drill ¹⁄₃₂-inch-diameter angled blade-entry holes through the lid at the inside corners of the design. Be sure to also drill at the correct direction (**9–17**).

6. Bevel-saw all around the outside profile of the interlocking knot design, with the table tilted left and feeding the stock clockwise (**9–18**).

9–14. Celtic box. The lid is made by a combination of scroll saw bevel-sawing and hand-carving (rounding-over) techniques.

7. Bevel-saw the inside pieces free, feeding the workpiece counterclockwise into the blade (**9–19**).

8. Temporarily press all pieces snugly in place (up or down) and lightly mark with a pencil the height of the relief along all of the sawn edges of the knot as shown in **9–20**.

9. Carve, shape, and sand the knot as shown in **9–21** to **9–23**.

10. Glue two or three layers together to make the box walls. If you cannot cut three layers at once, saw the third "ring" and glue it to the other two.

11. Cut the triangular box as shown in **9–24**.

12. Sand the walls as shown in **9–25**.

13. Cut the plywood pieces, one for the lid to keep it aligned and the other for the bottom (**9–26**).

14. Glue on the bottom and bevel back the edge. (See **9–15**.)

15. Sand and finish all surfaces.

16. Tack the plywood to the bottom side of the lid.

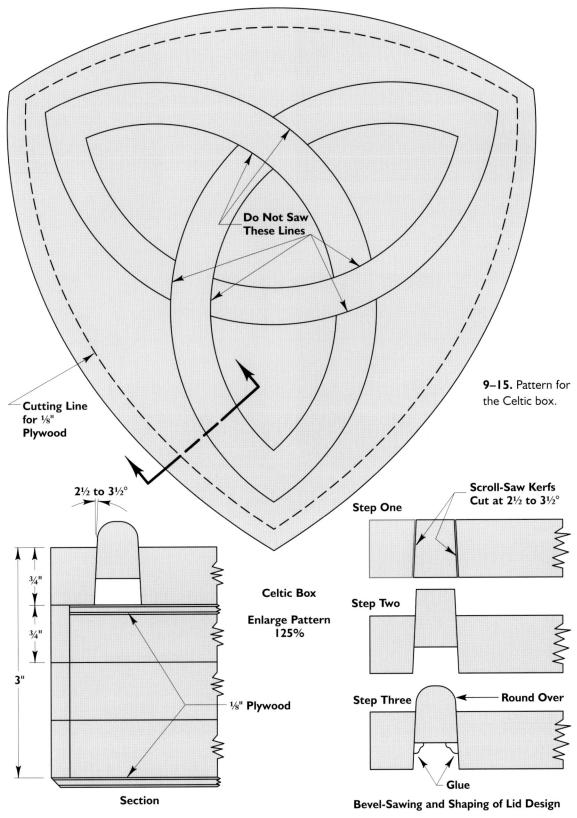

Do Not Saw These Lines

Cutting Line for ⅛" Plywood

9–15. Pattern for the Celtic box.

2½ to 3½°

¾"

¾"

3"

⅛" Plywood

Section

Celtic Box

Enlarge Pattern 125%

Scroll-Saw Kerfs Cut at 2½ to 3½°

Step One

Step Two

Step Three — **Round Over**

Glue

Bevel-Sawing and Shaping of Lid Design

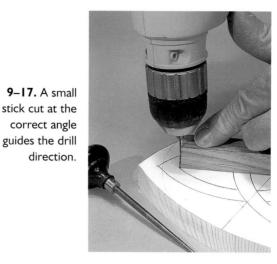

9–17. A small stick cut at the correct angle guides the drill direction.

9–16. Test bevel cuts made with the table tilted left. Feeding the work counterclockwise into the blade creates a recessed surface (left) and feeding clockwise will produce a cut piece raised in relief (right).

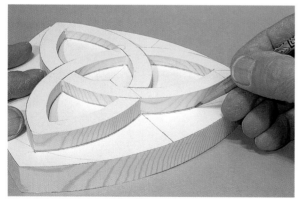

9–18. Bevel-sawing the outside perimeter of the Celtic knot. The saw table is tilted left and the work is fed clockwise into the blade.

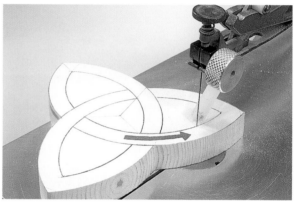

9–19. Cutting the inside triangular pieces. The saw table is tilted left and the work is now fed counterclockwise into the blade to create a recessed rather than a relief surface.

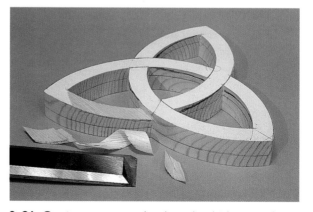

9–20. The bevel-sawing completed. The knot piece is now in relief to the background. Mark the height of relief to aid in carving and shaping the knot.

9–21. Carving to taper and reduce the thickness is done in six areas as shown. Here a flat chisel was used.

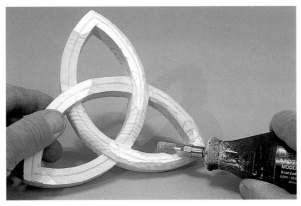

9–22. Rounding over the edges. Notice the freehand centerline (in red) drawn to guide hand-shaping.

9–23. Shaped and sanded parts glued in place get a final sanding with a flutter wheel. (See 9–15 for glue application.)

9–24. Sawing two glue-laminated layers to make the side walls.

9–25. Sanding all three layers.

9–26. Tracing the inside of the box on plywood, which is then sawn and tacked (without glue) under the lid to keep it aligned.

PERSONALIZED PROJECTS

Everyone loves to see their name cut from wood. This chapter offers three personalized projects: initial plaques, house numbers, and name signs. All involve making cutout letters and applying them to a prepared background. Also presented are several different finishing options. The most interesting and elegant is gold leaf, which is presented in the most elementary and workable manner.

GARGOYLE HOUSE NUMBERS

The plaque (**10–1** and **10–2**) is made from a single piece of 1 × 12-inch wood in whatever length is necessary to accommodate the quantity of numbers required. The fretwork gargoyle requires a piece of ⅛- to ⅜-inch-thick material that's 5½ × 8¼ inches. Use the same material to cut the 4-inch-high letters. Baltic-birch plywood is a good choice. The border is bevel-cut from the plaque edge and raised and glued (**10–3**).

GENERAL CONSTRUCTION TIPS:

1. Lay out the number patterns and, if necessary, modify the plaque and frame pattern accordingly.

2. Cut the gargoyle, numbers, and the outside shape of the plaque. Use a no. 9 ground blade and bevel-saw the one-piece border free with the table tilted left 2½ to 3½ degrees. Feed the stock into the blade in a counterclockwise direction while keeping the plaque to the left of the blade and the border to the right.

3. Use coarse abrasive and gently round over the edges of the border.

4. Prime and finish all pieces individually. Use metallic aerosol paint to coat the gargoyle, number, and border pieces. Gold leaf is also an option. Turn to page 163 for information on how to apply gold leaf. Do not finish the gluing surfaces of the plaque edge.

5. Carefully glue the border raised in relief (**10–4**).

6. Use brass wood screws and no. 16 × 1-inch brass escutcheon pins to attach the numbers and gargoyle, respectively.

10–1.
Gargoyle/house numbers.

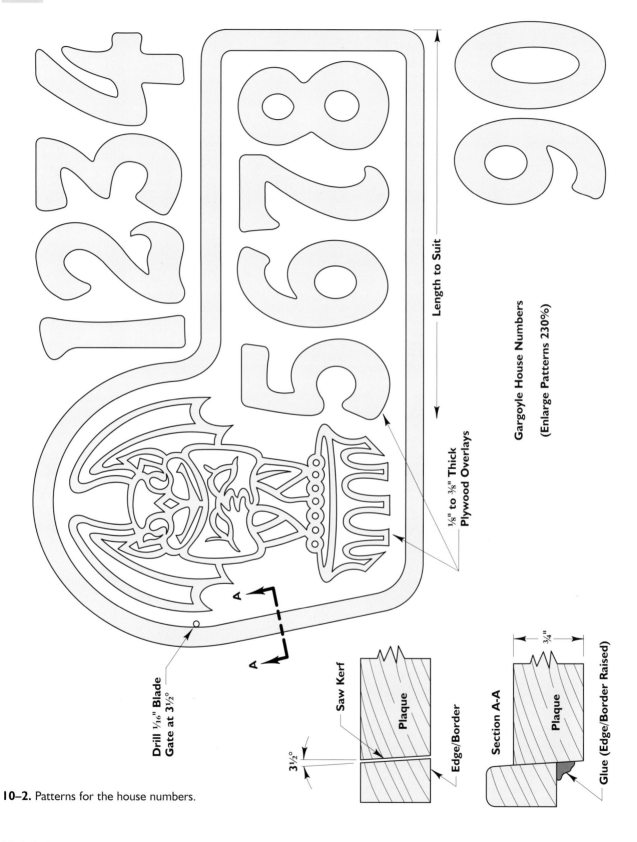

Length to Suit

⅛" to ⅜" Thick
Plywood Overlays

Gargoyle House Numbers
(Enlarge Patterns 230%)

Drill ¹⁄₁₆" Blade
Gate at 3½°

A
A

3½°

Saw Kerf

Plaque

Edge/Border

¾"

Section A-A

Plaque

Glue (Edge/Border Raised)

10–2. Patterns for the house numbers.

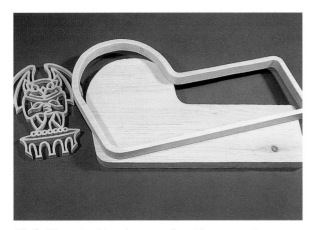

10–3. The raised border is made with one continuous bevel cut all around the plaque.

10–4. Moderate clamping pressure is necessary to eliminate the tendency of a gap from developing at this area when gluing the border in place.

INITIAL PLAQUES

These plaques (**10–5** to **10–7**) are elegant decorations for the den, family room, office, or they can be mounted to the front door. Three designs are provided in various levels of detail (**10–7**). Each plaque is made by gluing overlay border pieces to a backer. First prepare the pattern(s) to the desired size. Use ⅜- to ½-inch-thick material (Baltic-birch plywood) for backers and ⅛- to ¼-inch-thick material for the overlays. Stack-saw the outside edge profiles of the overlay border and backers when making design nos. 2 and 3. Then separate the pieces and complete sawing the interior of the overlay border piece only (**10–6**). Glue and finish as desired. Notice that the plaques shown in **10–5** were finished with gold leaf on the flat face surfaces only (not the edges). Refer to page 163 for gold-leafing instructions.

10–5. Initial plaques that feature overlays and a gold-leaf finish. The middle design can be lengthened from the centerline to make a long name or a house number plaque.

10–6. The outside perimeters of both the backer and overlays are stack-sawn together and then separated for sawing the inside openings.

10–7. Patterns for the initial plaques.

Overlays

Design No. 2

Design No. 1

**Initial Plaques
Designs by Dirk Boelman**

(Enlarge or Size as Desired)

Design No. 3

NAME/NUMBER SIGN

This project (**10–8** and **10–9**) provides an elegant name or house number sign. Like the initial plaques discussed previously, the plaque design has a separately cut and applied overlay border. *Note*: The initial plaque pattern design no. 1 (**10–7**) can easily be modified (extended vertically) to make an elongated name sign similar to the one shown in **10–8**.

First develop and size the pattern(s) as desired. Make four photocopies, one for cutting the detail in each end of the backer and the border. Use ¼- to ½-inch material as desired. Three-eighth-inch Baltic-birch plywood was used for all of the parts of the sign shown in **10–8**. Glue the border to the backer, attach the letters, and finish and/or apply gold leaf (**10–10** to **10–15**).

BASIC GOLD-LEAF TECHNIQUES

Gold leaf is available as the pure material (expensive) or as composition leaf, which consists of cheaper alloys. Test/experiment with the following procedures before adopting them for your project:

1. To keep it simple, plan to gold-leaf flat, facing surfaces only.

2. Sand raw wood surfaces to at least 400–600 grit.

3. Prime and paint surfaces, sanding between coats of paint.

4. Wet-sand painted surfaces using wet/dry silicon abrasives with a little water, as a lubricant, and working to 600 grit (**10–10**).

5. Wipe everything thoroughly clean with a damp rag. Allow it to dry.

6. Apply "size" very carefully, coating only surfaces that are to receive the gold leaf. The size is actually a clear adhesive. Use a high-quality artist's brush (**10–11**).

7. Test for "tack" using your knuckle as shown in **10–12**. Lightly drag it over the surface. If size sticks to your knuckle, it is still too wet. When the size is properly dry, your knuckle should make a squeaky sound. Best results favor a drier rather than a wet size coating.

8. Apply the leaf (**10–13** to **10–15**). The leaf comes mounted on tissue paper. Press the gold leaf onto the prepared surface(s) with the side of your hand as shown in **10–14**. Overlap previously laid leaf about ⅛ inch.

9. When applying leaf, do not worry about open gaps. Simply patch these in later. Overlaps and seams will not be visible (**10–15**).

10. Remove excess leaf with a soft cloth. Lightly burnish the gilded surfaces with balls of moistened cotton.

11. For added protection, apply a varnish top coat. This is only an option if real gold leaf was used. Applying a coat of varnish is, however, strongly recommended if the less-expensive "composition leaf" was used.

10–8. This name sign features an overlay border piece and gold-leaf accents.

10–9. Patterns for the name/number sign.

Note: Enlarge or Size Patterns to Suit

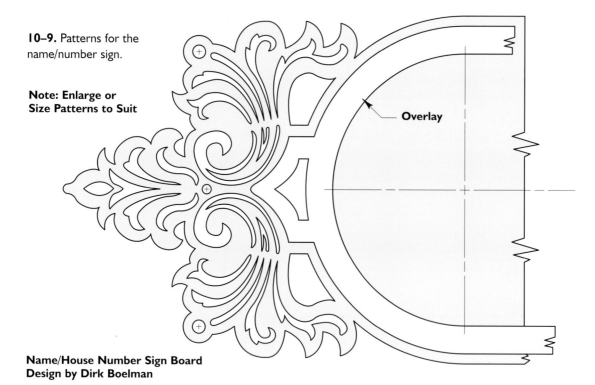

Overlay

Name/House Number Sign Board Design by Dirk Boelman

ABCDEFGHIJK
LMNOPQRSTU
VWXYZabcdefg
hijklmnopqrstuv
wxyz1234567890

10–10. Wet-sanding.

10–11. Carefully brush on the "size" (adhesive) for the gold leaf.

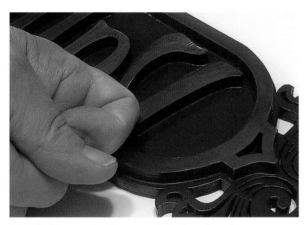

10–12. Testing the dryness of the "size" with your knuckle.

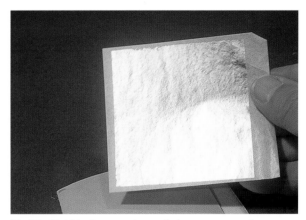

10–13. Gold leaf comes in small sheets mounted to tissue paper.

10–14. Laying down the gold leaf. Use the side of your hand to apply moderate pressure. Apply each piece overlapping the previous one about ⅛ inch.

10–15. Use fingertips to transfer gold leaf to small areas, to fill in voids, or to cover small, open spaces. one about ⅛ inch.

LOGSCAPES

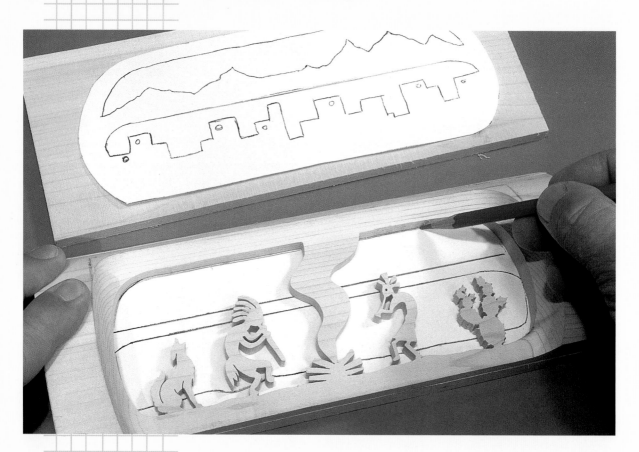

LOGSCAPE PROJECTS

These projects involve a system of layering multiple silhouettes to create a dimensional scene that appears as if it were magically carved within a solid log. The process, perfected and crafted by Dean Larson, requires a band saw and a natural or laminated log-like chunk of wood that finishes 4 inches wide (high). This simulated "half" log is easily created by laminating three layers of 5/16-inch-thick wood slices to a fourth "window" piece that is 1¼ inch thick. Band-sawn slices (**11–2** and **11–3**), cut from a real log or one-piece lumber of sufficient size, look better than separately selected pieces glued together because the color and grain patterns will be consistent.

Three different designs are provided. Each has a slightly different length, so prepare the patterns and select the stock accordingly.

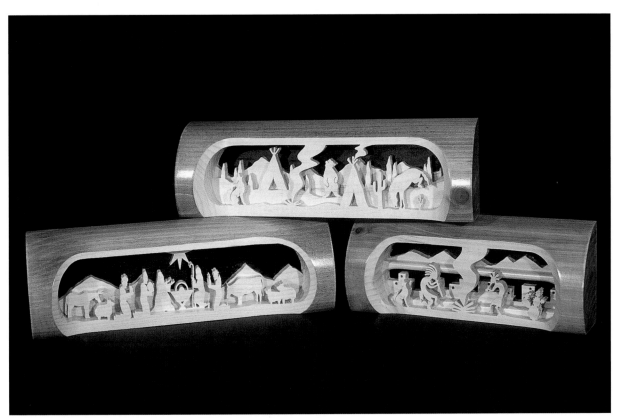

11–1. Logscapes by Dean Larson involve systematically layering several simple scroll-sawn silhouettes together in an assembly that simulates a carved log. See pages 170 to 173 for patterns.

GENERAL CONSTRUCTION TIPS:

1. Prepare a blank to the end-view specifications given on the patterns (**11–8** and **11–9**).

2. Draw a vertical centerline and some surface guidelines for making the window band-saw cut shown in process (**11–2**).

3. Cut the window piece free with a resaw cut as shown in **11–3** and prepare the three remaining thin slices in the same manner.

4. Apply the patterns so they are centered on the window piece (**11–4**) and on the two other silhouette slabs.

5. If necessary, modify the scroll saw cutting lines of the window pattern. Making slight changes to the pattern's inside perimeter line will produce a uniform window "frame" width all around as shown in **11–5**.

6. Cut out the window silhouette with the scroll saw.

7. Place the sawn window silhouette over silhouette pattern no. 2. Check and make any necessary cutting line changes (**11–6**).

8. Scroll-saw silhouette pattern no. 2.

9. Use the sawn silhouette no. 2 to make any changes that may be necessary on the pattern of silhouette no. 3. Then cut it out.

10. Paint the front, exposed area of the backer black, protecting the gluing areas with masking tape.

11. Glue all of the layers together. Sand the outer surfaces.

12. Stain the outside surfaces a fruitwood color and apply a coat of clear satin finish (**11–7**).

Note: See **11–10** and **11–11** for two additional logscape patterns.

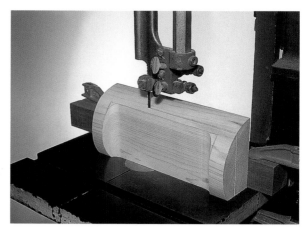

11–2. Freehand-sawing the window recess into the curved surface. Notice the red guidelines made to help ensure cutting accuracy.

11–3. Resawing to free the window piece. Cut the piece to a thickness of approximately ⁵⁄₁₆ inch at the thinnest area.

11–4. Apply the window silhouette pattern; center it on the workpiece.

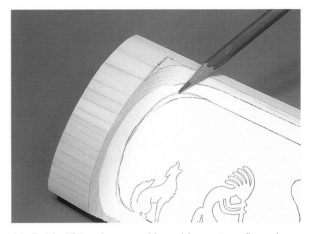

11–5. Modifying the curved lines (shown in red) on the inside of the "window" pattern. This may be necessary to ensure that the resulting frame-like surfaces will be the same width all around.

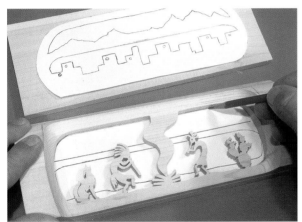

11–6. The window silhouette becomes a pattern to modify the perimeter line of the inside opening of silhouette no. 2.

11–7. Close-up of completed logscape.

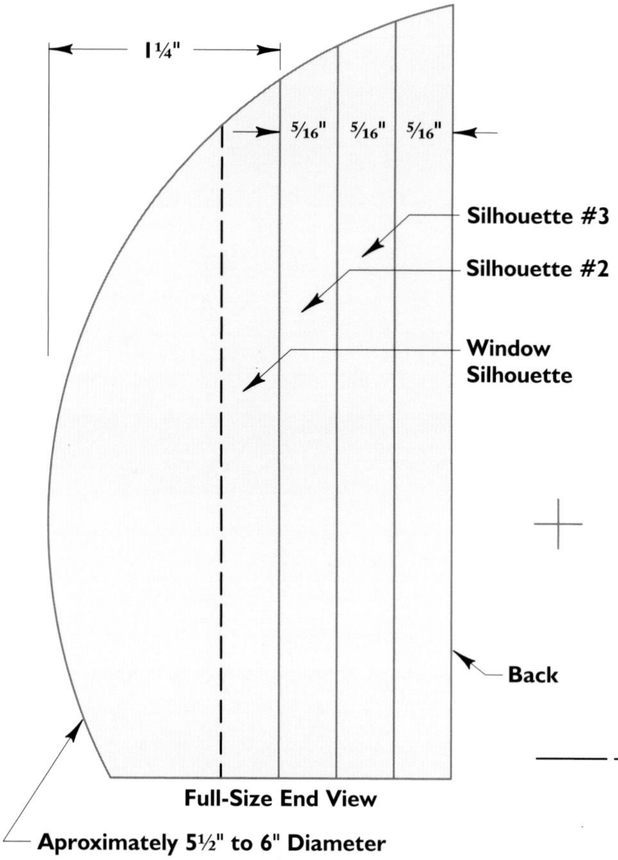

1¼"

5/16" 5/16" 5/16"

Silhouette #3

Silhouette #2

Window
Silhouette

Back

Full-Size End View

Aproximately 5½" to 6" Diameter

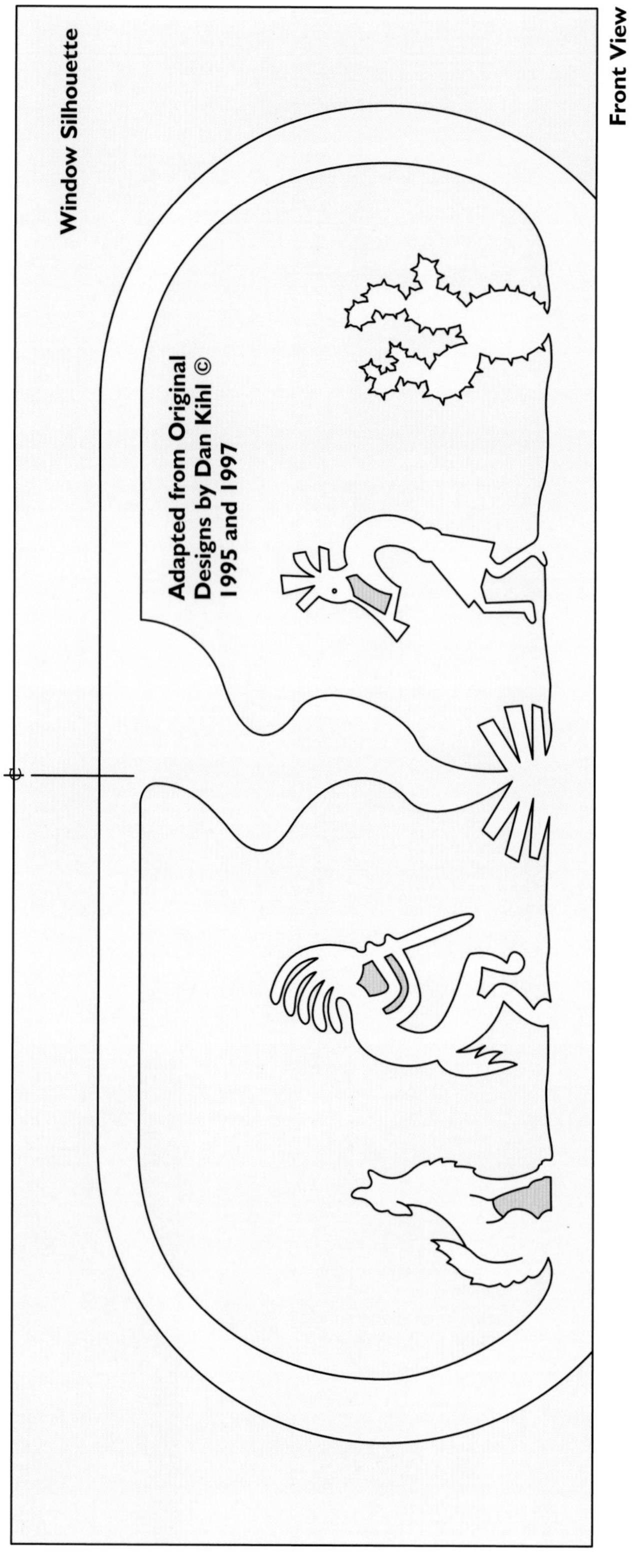

**Southwest Logscape
Design Concept by Dean Larson**

Enlarge Window Silhouette Pattern 125%

Window Silhouette

Front View

**Adapted from Original
Designs by Dan Kihl ©
1995 and 1997**

11–8. Pattern for the southwest logscape.

11–9. Patterns for the southwest logscape.

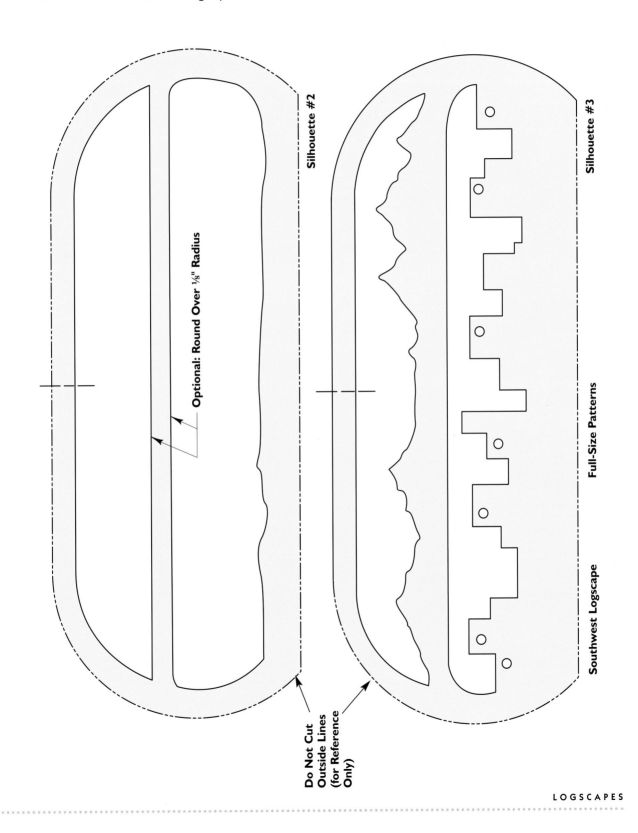

Silhouette #2

Optional: Round Over ⅛" Radius

Do Not Cut Outside Lines (for Reference Only)

Silhouette #3

Full-Size Patterns

Southwest Logscape

11–10. Patterns for nativity logscape.

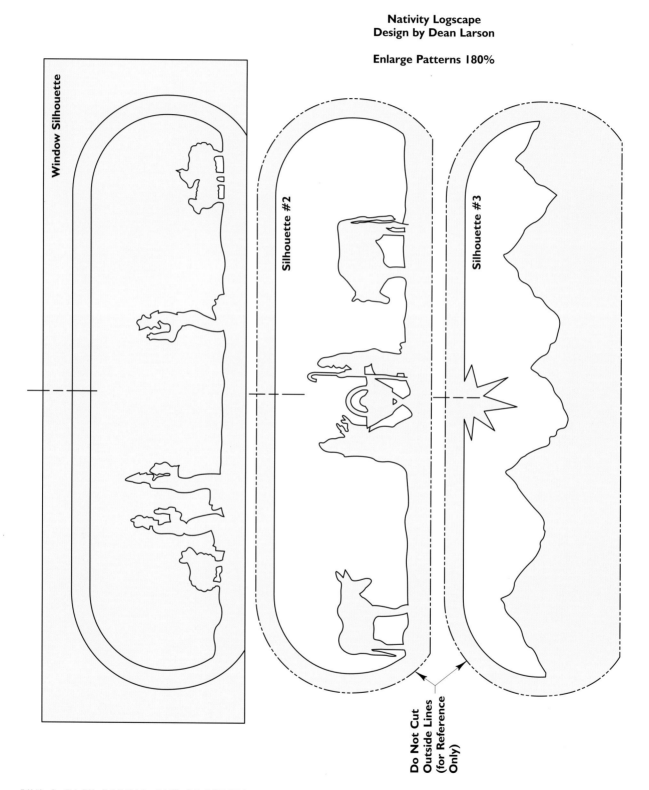

**Nativity Logscape
Design by Dean Larson**

Enlarge Patterns 180%

Window Silhouette

Silhouette #2

Silhouette #3

Do Not Cut
Outside Lines
(for Reference
Only)

11–11. Patterns for western logscape.

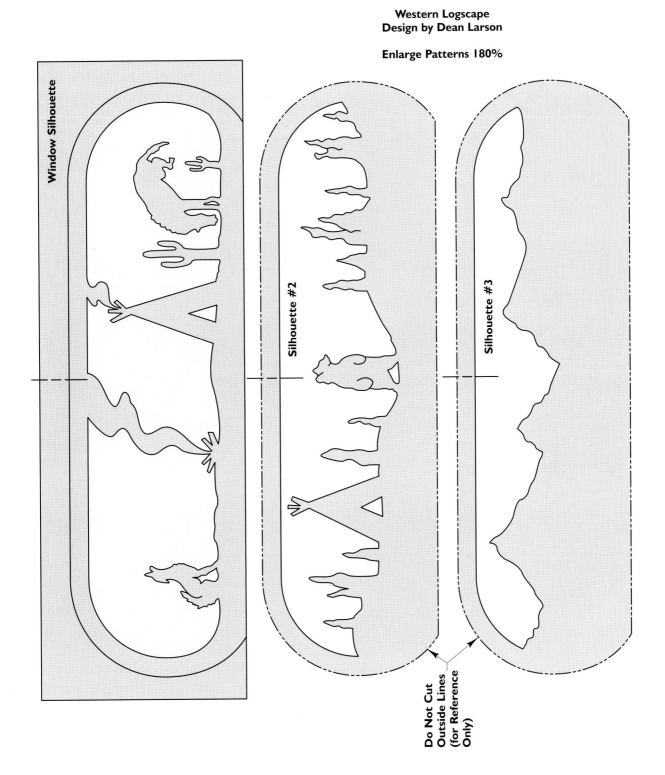

Western Logscape
Design by Dean Larson

Enlarge Patterns 180%

Window Silhouette

Silhouette #2

Silhouette #3

Do Not Cut
Outside Lines
(for Reference
Only)

MISCELLANEOUS HOME ACCESSORIES

12

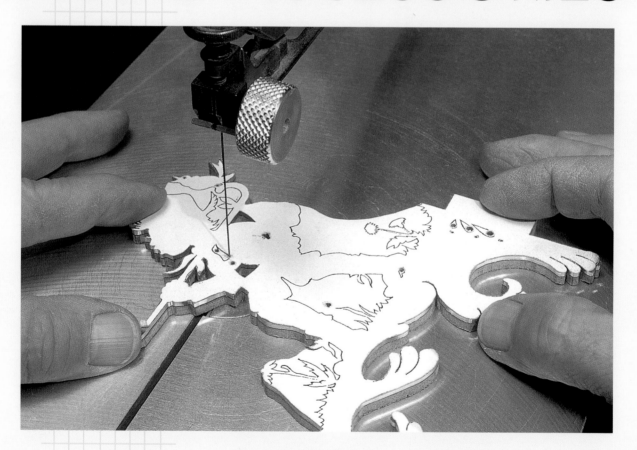

This chapter includes a number of different projects that are essentially very easy to make and distinct departures from the ordinary.

GOLF BALL DISPLAY RACK

This project as designed (**12–1** and **12–2**) holds 29 golf balls. The back is made from ⅛- to ½-inch-thick 12½ × 16¼-inch plywood. The design can easily be modified to hold more or fewer balls, adding or subtracting 2¼ inches (equivalent to a row of five balls) at the bottom. Finish the plaque and overlays as desired. Two real tees support each ball. They are available in a rainbow of colors or a natural finish. Tee sizes vary, so be sure to obtain all 58 pieces from the same source. Then test-drill the optimum hole size, which should require a moderately firm fit. Give each tee a drop of glue before inserting.

12–1. This golf ball display rack is made from birch plywood and real golf tees.

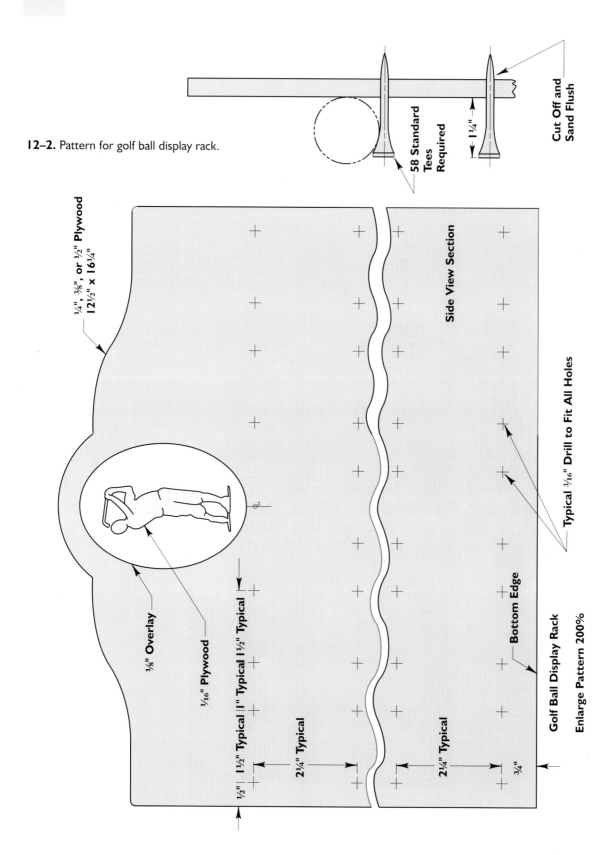

12–2. Pattern for golf ball display rack.

Cut Off and Sand Flush

58 Standard Tees Required

1¼"

¼", ⅜", or ½" Plywood
12½" x 16¼"

Side View Section

Typical ³/₁₆" Drill to Fit All Holes

⅛" Overlay

¹/₁₆" Plywood

Bottom Edge

Golf Ball Display Rack
Enlarge Pattern 200%

½" | 1½" Typical | 1" Typical 1½" Typical |

2¼" Typical

2¼" Typical

¾"

SCONCE

This project (**12–3** to **12–7**) combines basic scroll work with a little turning to make the simple candle cups. The pattern is best enlarged 135 percent as recommended to be proportional with standard candles. Use ¼ to ½-inch-thick plywood that's 8 × 16¾ inches for the back. Two pieces are needed for the bracket. One is ¼ × 2 × 2¾ inches, and the other ½ × 1½ x 3 inches. Turn the candle cup as specified or purchase one ready-made. Cut all pieces and smooth and assemble them as desired. Optional faux patina finishes applied to the wood will give the project(s) a metallic look; otherwise, finish the projects as desired. See **12–4** and **12–5** for some examples and tips.

12–3. Sconce design made of plywood with a rust patina finish and details to simulate metal.

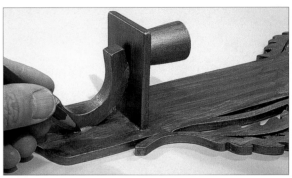

12–4. Obviously visible beads of heavy-viscosity instant or epoxy adhesive simulate a weld that adds to the realistic look of metal. Here, a metallic base coat of liquid brass has been applied, preparing it for the patina rust solution.

12–5. A close-up look at another metallic finish. This is a burgundy patina solution applied over a liquid copper coating using a plastic bottle and spray mister.

12–6. Pattern for the sconce.

⅛" or ¼" Thick Material

Sconce

Enlarge Pattern 135%

12–7. Patterns for the sconce.

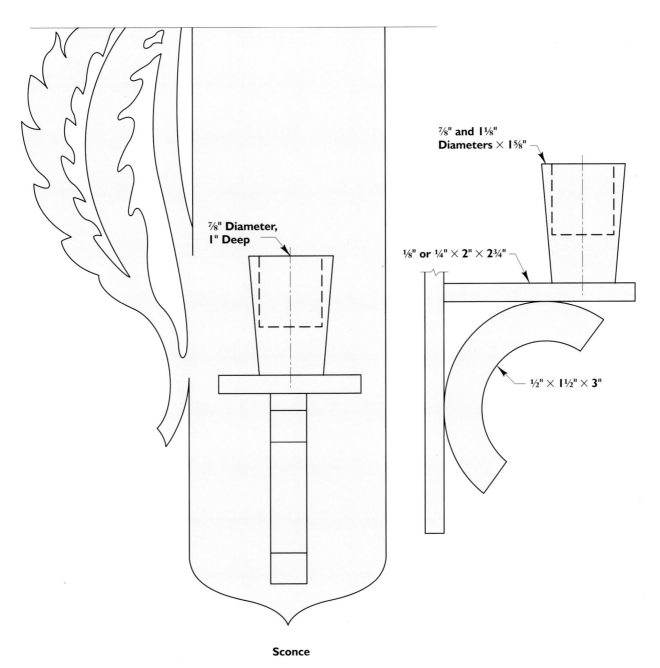

⁷⁄₈" **and** 1¹⁄₈"
Diameters × 1⁵⁄₈"

⁷⁄₈" **Diameter,**
1" **Deep**

¹⁄₈" **or** ¹⁄₄" × 2" × 2³⁄₄"

½" × 1½" × 3"

Sconce

Enlarge Patterns 135%

TRIVETS

To make the trivets shown in **12–8**, enlarge the pattern(s) to suit and cut the pattern(s) from ¼- to ½-inch-thick material such as solid hardwood, plywood, Corian, plastic, or perhaps soft brass. The edges should be rounded over around both the top or bottom perimeters to make them more user-friendly.

12–8. Patterns for trivets.

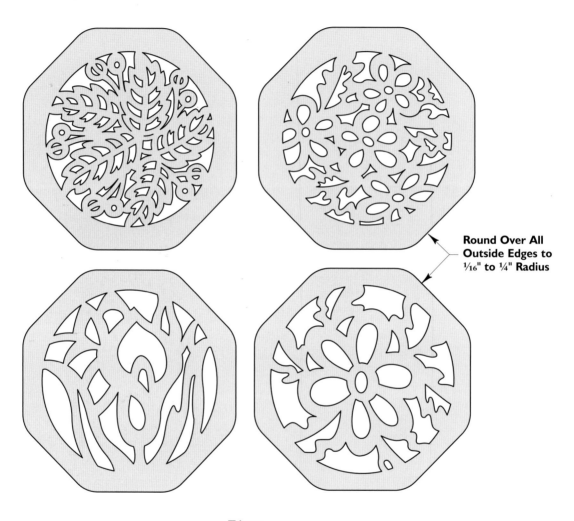

Round Over All Outside Edges to ¹⁄₁₆" to ¼" Radius

Trivets

Enlarge Patterns 350 to 370%

WALL HANGER

This project (**12–9** and **12–10**) is a Karl Gutbrod design combining basic woodworking with some scroll saw metal-cutting. Use this project for hanging special decorative ornaments, a flowerpot, or the family dinner bell, which can be purchased from a department store. The required materials are:

- *One piece of brass or copper: 16 or 14 gauge x 5½ x 6½ inches*

- *One ¾ × 1⅛ × 7½-inch piece*

- *Two ¼ × 1¼ × 3¾-inch pieces, for the roof*

- *Two ¼ × 1 × 2⅞-inch pieces, for the roof brackets*

- *One screw-hole button: ⅜ inch in diameter*

- *Two pins (wire brads): ¾ inch × 18 gauge*

GENERAL CONSTRUCTION TIPS:

1. Use metal-cutting blades with 42 to 56 teeth per inch. Lubricate blade with beeswax.

2. Buff the metal with steel wool thoroughly before applying the pattern and cutting and finishing the metal.

3. Support the metal on a piece of ¼-inch scrap plywood to provide better sawing control.

4. Carefully cut the slot in the vertical "post," matching the pattern lines to the thickness of metal used.

5. Make the roof miter cuts on a disc sander or hand-cut them carefully with a backsaw.

6. Prefinish the metal before assembly in any finish desired. Options include coloring it with an aerosol spray, leaving it natural with a polish and varnishing the top coat, or finishing with a patina as shown in **12–12**.

7. Pin the metal to the post using two wire brads driven into drilled holes (no. 56 drill bit).

12–9. A wall hanger made from ¹⁄₃₂-inch copper (16 or 14 gauge) with a patina finish and natural pine.

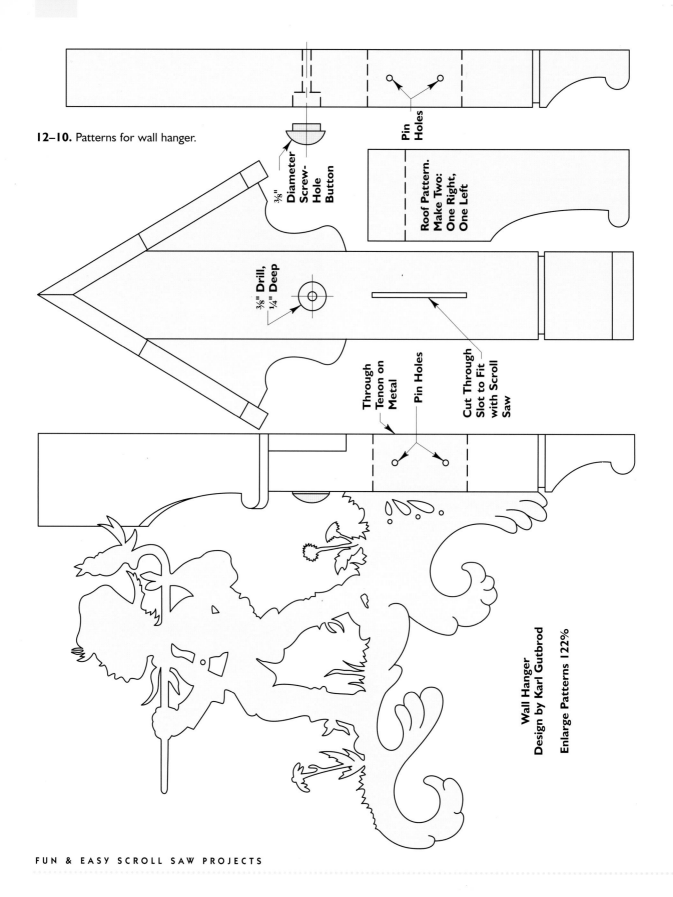

12–10. Patterns for wall hanger.

3/8" Diameter Screw-Hole Button

Pin Holes

Roof Pattern. Make Two: One Right, One Left

3/8" Drill, 1/4" Deep

Through Tenon on Metal

Pin Holes

Cut Through Slot to Fit with Scroll Saw

Wall Hanger Design by Karl Gutbrod

Enlarge Patterns 122%

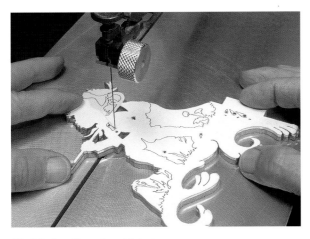

12–11. Scroll-sawing thick sheet copper.

12–12. Applying a patina solution to the cleaned copper surfaces with a sponge.

STACKED RING BOWL

Without any waste, a 9-inch-square board will produce the undulating stacked ring bowl shown in **12–13** to **12–16**. Use any solid wood ½ inch, ¾ inch, or more in thickness. Two sets of patterns are provided (**12–15** and **12–16**) that are essentially the same, just slightly different in size. Whichever set you use, make two photocopies and butt them together to complete the full set of ring patterns (**12–14**).

The fun part of this project is to interject your own creativity. Do this by selecting and interchanging rings from both pattern sets into one project. You can also combine different thicknesses and colors of woods. Cut out the rings and sand the sawn edges slightly round. Assemble the project with droplets of instant glue. Build up the rings by rotating each successive ring 22½ degrees.

Use ⅛- or ¹⁄₁₆-inch-thick plywood for the bottom. Cut it to match the shape of the bottom ring. Bevel the edge of the bottom back so it is not visible and glue it to the bottom ring. Finish the assembled project with peanut or mineral oil if it will be used with food.

12–13. Stacked undulating ring bowl developed by Joan West.

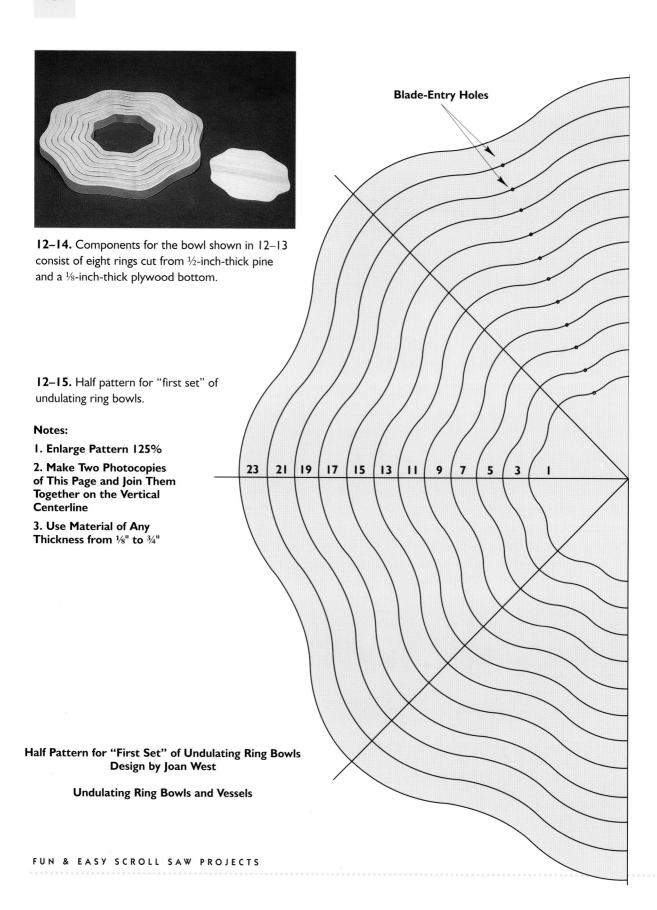

12–14. Components for the bowl shown in 12–13 consist of eight rings cut from ½-inch-thick pine and a ⅛-inch-thick plywood bottom.

12–15. Half pattern for "first set" of undulating ring bowls.

Notes:

1. Enlarge Pattern 125%

2. Make Two Photocopies of This Page and Join Them Together on the Vertical Centerline

3. Use Material of Any Thickness from ⅛" to ¾"

Blade-Entry Holes

23   21   19   17   15   13   11   9   7   5   3   1

**Half Pattern for "First Set" of Undulating Ring Bowls
Design by Joan West**

Undulating Ring Bowls and Vessels

12–16. Half-pattern for "second set" of undulating ring bowls.

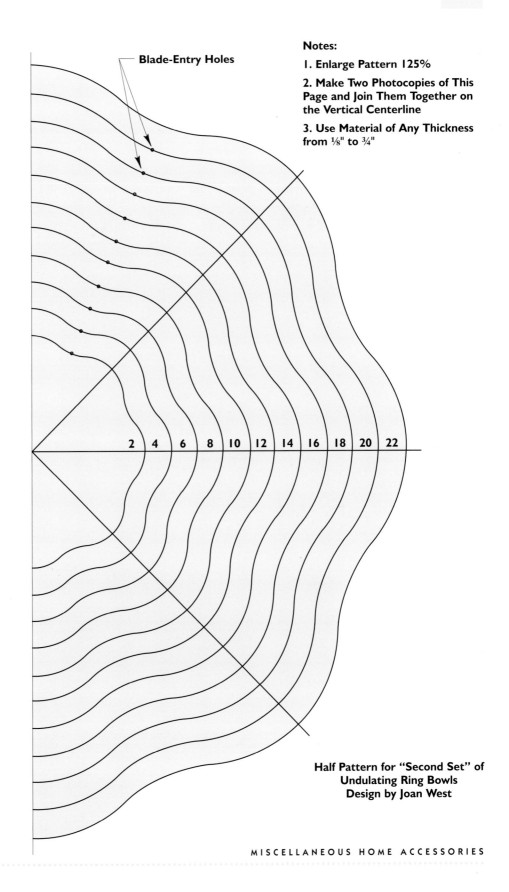

Blade-Entry Holes

Notes:

1. Enlarge Pattern 125%

2. Make Two Photocopies of This Page and Join Them Together on the Vertical Centerline

3. Use Material of Any Thickness from ⅛" to ¾"

2   4   6   8   10   12   14   16   18   20   22

Half Pattern for "Second Set" of Undulating Ring Bowls Design by Joan West

SCULPTURED WALL PLANTER

This wall planter (**12–17** to **12–21**) combines fundamental scroll-sawing and routing operations on 20 pieces of wood. A single 1 × 8-inch softwood board six feet in length reduced to a thickness of ½ or ⅝ inch is required, or multiple pieces of smaller scraps can be used. The advantage of cutting all pieces from one board, however, is color and grain uniformity. Make two of each part, stack-sawing every pair to save time. Lay out all pieces so the grain direction will be vertical. Cut out the necessary parts and rout the outside edges with a ¼ radius (**12–18**). The straight wall-side edges of each piece, however, are *not* rounded over. Sand and carefully glue these pieces together in appropriate sequence. Drill a mounting hole through the wall-side surface and finish the project as desired. Cut off plastic soda bottles to make liners that will hold water for freshly cut flowers or plants.

12–17. This sculptured wall planter in southern pine designed and crafted by Joan West is classically elegant and easily constructed.

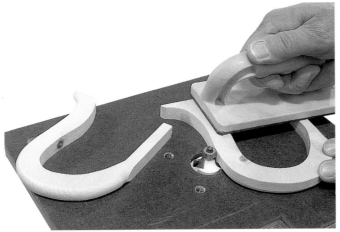

12–18. A ¼-inch round-over bit with a router table is used to shape the outside edges of the ½-inch-thick cutouts. Notice that the routing stops at the straight-line areas as shown by the completed piece at the left.

**Wall Planter
Designs by Joan West**

12–19. Patterns for the wall planter.

Enlarge Patterns 125%

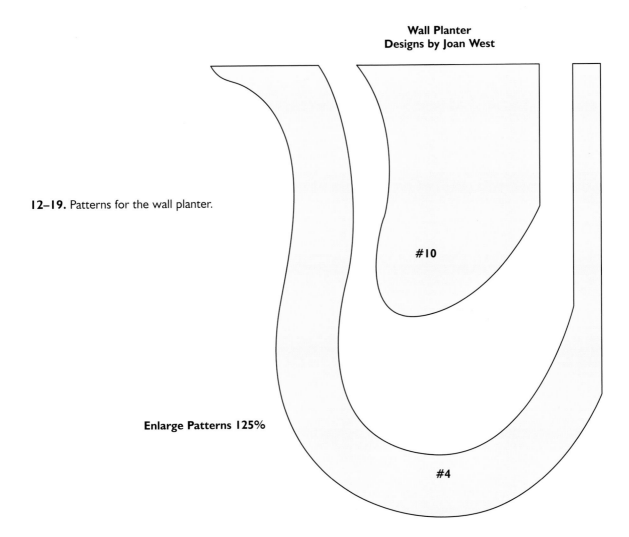

#10

#4

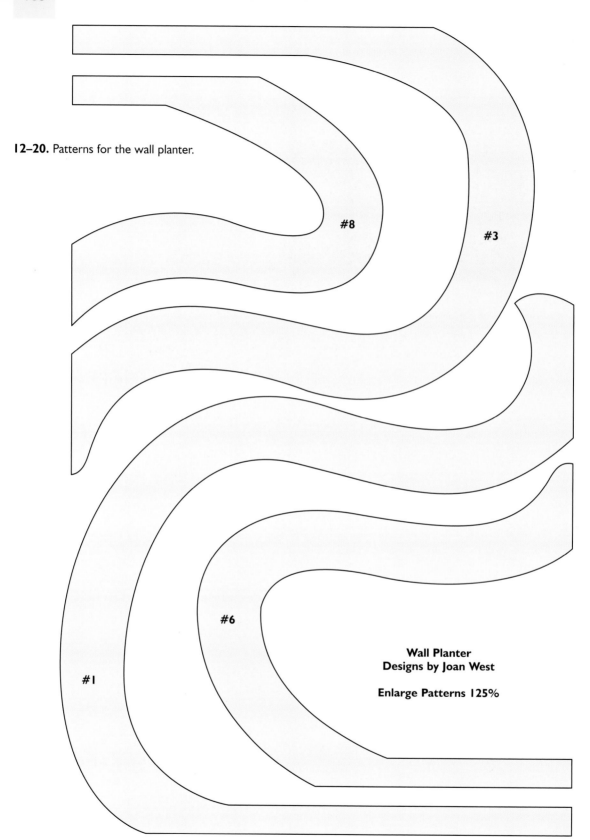

12–20. Patterns for the wall planter.

#8

#3

#6

#1

Wall Planter
Designs by Joan West

Enlarge Patterns 125%

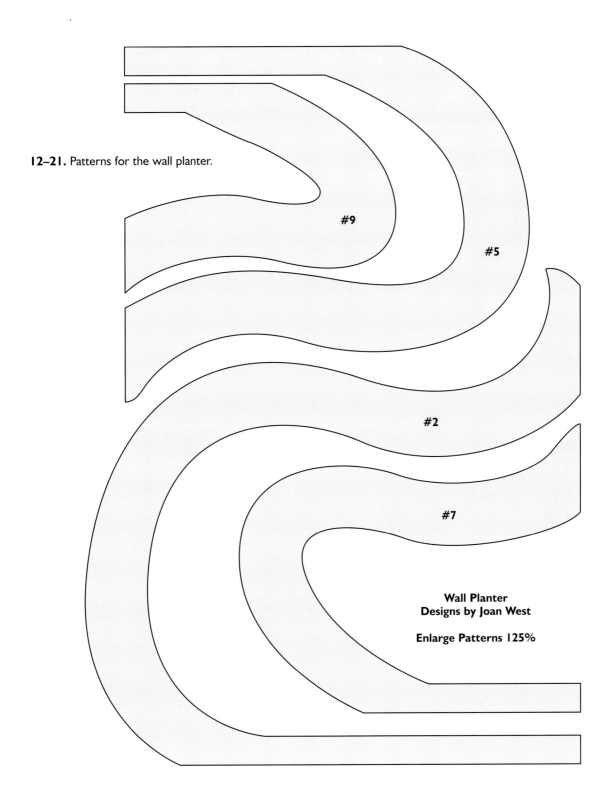

12–21. Patterns for the wall planter.

#9

#5

#2

#7

**Wall Planter
Designs by Joan West**

Enlarge Patterns 125%

METRIC EQUIVALENCY CHART

Inches to Millimeters and Centimeters

MM=Millimeters   CM=Centimeters

Inches	MM	CM	Inches	CM	Inches	CM
⅛	3	0.3	9	22.9	30	76.2
¼	6	0.6	10	25.4	31	78.7
⅜	10	1.0	11	27.9	32	81.3
½	13	1.3	12	30.5	33	83.8
⅝	16	1.6	13	33.0	34	86.4
¾	19	1.9	14	35.6	35	88.9
⅞	22	2.2	15	38.1	36	91.4
1	25	2.5	16	40.6	37	94.0
1¼	32	3.2	17	43.2	38	96.5
1½	38	3.8	18	45.7	39	99.1
1¾	44	4.4	19	48.3	48	101.6
2	51	5.1	20	50.8	41	104.1
2½	64	6.4	21	53.3	42	106.7
3	76	7.6	22	55.9	43	109.2
3½	89	8.9	23	58.4	44	111.8
4	102	10.2	24	61.0	45	114.3
4½	114	11.4	25	63.5	46	116.8
5	127	12.7	26	66.0	47	119.4
6	152	15.2	27	68.6	48	121.9

INDEX

Acrobat sculpture, 26, 28
Acrylic
  acrobat sculpture, 26, 28
  dancer, 32
  mirror, 110
  as project material, 7
  "Twelve Days of Christmas," 66–68
Alien bat, 48
Alien reflector, 34–35
Angel ornaments, 56, 59, 61, 63, 64–65

Bell ornaments, 57–58
Bird and flower wreath, 87, 89
Bird of paradise, 107
Blades, scroll saw
  spiral, 131
  threading, 12
  types of, 8, 9
Bodie Island house, 40–41
Bookmarks, 17
Bowls, stacked ring, 183, 184–185
Boxes
  Celtic, 154–157
  heart, 152–153
  overlaid tissue, 148, 151
  secret storage book, 147, 148
Brass, cutting, 25

Candlesticks, 140–145
Cats and dogs, 90
Cedars on Lake Michigan shoreline, 103
Celtic cross, 83–85
Christmas silhouettes, 70–71
Clocks
  Chevy, 125, 126
  cormorants, 128, 130
  dragon, 128, 129
  mini fretwork, 125, 127
  oval, 131, 132
  slab, 131, 133
Corian
  cutability of, 8
  eye sculpture, 32, 33
  kokopelli sculpture, 30–31
  unicorn, 26
Cormorants clock, 128, 130
Cranes, 113
Crosses
  Celtic, 83, 84–85
  fretwork, 76, 77–78
  key-chain and pendant, 73, 74–75, 76
  with overlays, 79, 80–82, 83
Cutouts
  bird, 130

fretwork, 95,
inside, 12
shaping outside edges of, 187
small, 22
stylized horse, 95, 96
window topper, 97

Dancer sculpture, 32, 33
Deer scene, 100, 102
Dimensional butterflies, 36–37
Display rack, 175, 176
Dove ornaments, 52–53, 57, 58
Dragon clock, 128, 129
Dust, extracting, 9

Eagle, 91
Easter eggs, 49
Eiffel Towel, 42–43
Elvis cutout, 108, 109
Eye sculpture, 32, 33

Fabric dye, 51
Fans for workshop, 9
Fantasy creatures, 114
Finishes
  dip, 51
  for holiday ornaments, 45
  patina, 7, 8, 32, 8, 177, 181
  textured stone, 79, 83
Fish cutout, 106, 108
Flaming cross, 75, 76
Fluorescent alien, 34–35
Flutter wheel, 139, 150
Fretwork projects
  clock, 125, 127
  crosses, 76–78
  ornaments, 54–56, 59, 60
  shelves, 117, 118–121
  stained-glass angels, 64–65
  stick ornaments, 50
  Viking, 92

Gargoyle house numbers, 159, 160, 161
Gazelle, 18, 19
Giant panda, 100, 101
Giraffe, 93
Glory cross, 75
Gold-leaf techniques, 163, 164–165
Golf ball display rack, 175, 176
Golfer, 103

Hearing protection, 9
Heart designs, 45–47, 152–153
Holiday ornaments, 45–71

Horses, 95, 110–112
House numbers, 159, 160, 161
Hummingbird, 91, 151

Initial plaques, 161, 162
Inside cutouts, 12

Jazz angels ornaments, 61
Jewelry, 22–25

Key chains, 21, 73–75
Kokopelli sculpture, 30–31

Letter openers, 18, 20
Lion, 105
Logscapes, 166–173

Magnifying light, 9
Marilyn cutout, 108, 109
Materials and finishes, 7, 8
Mini fretwork clock, 125, 127

Name/number sign, 163–165
Nativity logscape, 172
Nativity ornament, 60
Nine Ladies Dancing, 69

Old German Christmas silhouettes,
  70–71
Ornaments, 44–71
Oval clock, 131, 132
Owl reflector, 34

Packaging tape, 12, 13
Paper clips, 17, 18, 19
Partridge in a Pear Tree ornament, 62
Pattern techniques, 10, 11
Pendant crosses, 73–76
Phantom lady, 98
Pierced silhouettes, 87, 88, 134
Plaques
  gargoyle house numbers, 159, 160, 161
  initial, 161, 162
  time and temperature, 137–139
  wall, 74, 76
Prefontaine, Steve, 134, 135
Proportional scale, 10
Protractor, 11

Reflectors, 34

Safety techniques, 9
Sanding, 12, 13, 139
Saw table, adjusting, 11

Scandinavian stick ornaments, 50–51
Sconce, 177–179
Scroll saws
  preparing, 10, 11
  types of, 8
Scroll tops, 15
Sculptures
  acrylic acrobat, 26, 28
  eye, 32, 33
  horse, 110, 111, 112
  kokopelli, 30–31
  "Love," 45–47
  unicorn, 26, 27
  "wing," 26, 29
Secret storage book, 147, 148
Shamrock designs, 47
Shelves, 117–123
Shoreline, 103
Sign, 163–165
Silhouettes
  deer, 99
  old German, 70–71

pierced, 87, 88
  sports clock, 134
Slab clock, 131, 133
Soccer shelf, 122–123
Southwest logscape, 170–171
Sports clock, 134–136
Stacked ring bowl, 183, 184–185
Stack-sawing
  overlays, 83
  techniques, 11, 12
  tongue depressors, 50
Stack segmented ornaments, 50, 56–58
Stained-glass ornaments, 64–65
Standing gazelle, 18, 19
Stick ornaments, 50–51

Three ladies, 115
Thunderbird, 94
Tiger, 104
Time and temperature plaque, 137–139
Tissue box, 148, 151
Tongue depressors, 50

Transfer tool, 122
Trivets, 180
"Twelve Days of Christmas" ornament,
  66–69

Unicorn sculpture, 26, 27

Viking, 92

Walking fish, 38–39
Wall hanger, 181–182, 183
Wall planter, 186–189
Wall plaques
  cross, 74, 76
  stylized horse, 95, 96
  time and temperature, 137–139
Western logscape, 172
Window topper cutout, 97
"Wings" sculpture 26, 29
Wolf, 106
Workshop calipers, 16

ABOUT THE AUTHOR

Patrick Spielman is the leading author on woodworking throughout the world with over 65 books published, including the best-selling Router Handbook *and* Scroll Saw Pattern Book, *which have each sold over one million copies. A graduate of the University of Wisconsin–Stout, he has taught high school and vocational woodworking in Wisconsin public schools for 27 years. Patrick, with the assistance of his family, owned and operated a wood product manufacturing company for 20 years. Most recently, he published and distributed Home Workshop News, a bimonthly newsletter/magazine dedicated to scroll-sawing. Patrick and his wife Patricia currently own and operate Spielman's Wood Works and Spielman's Kid Works, two gift galleries located in northeastern Wisconsin that feature quality products made from wood.*

Over the course of Patrick's teaching and woodworking careers, he has invented hundreds of jigs, fixtures, and woodworking aids. He has served as a technical consultant and designer for a major tool manufacturer and he continues to pioneer new and exciting techniques for woodworkers as he has done for more than 45 years.